SCOTTISH SPECTRES

Here is a ghoulish collection of over two hundred hauntings from the length and breadth of Scotland. Whilst castles, old inns and pubs are the usual residences of spirits, there are sightings of spectres at some rather more unusual locations such as hospitals, ships, lighthouses, supermarkets, theatres, coalmines, restaurants and even toilets! There is the ghostly presence of a surgeon who haunts the hospital where he once worked, the disruptive poltergeist at a supermarket, the restaurant which echoes to the sounds of long-forgotten children, and a prison frequented by the spirit of a hanged man who suffered a most gruesome death — and much, much more.

DANE LOVE

◆

SCOTTISH SPECTRES

Complete and Unabridged

ULVERSCROFT
Leicester

First published in Great Britain in 2001 by
Robert Hale Limited
London

First Large Print Edition
published 2003
by arrangement with
Robert Hale Limited
London

The moral right of the author has been asserted

British Library CIP Data

Love, Dane
    Scottish spectres.—Large print ed.—
    Ulverscroft large print series: non-fiction
    1. Ghosts—Scotland 2. Apparitions—Scotland
    3. Haunted places—Scotland 4. Large type books
    I. Title
    133.1'09411

    ISBN 0–7089–4789–1

Published by
F. A. Thorpe (Publishing)
Anstey, Leicestershire

Set by Words & Graphics Ltd.
Anstey, Leicestershire
Printed and bound in Great Britain by
T. J. International Ltd., Padstow, Cornwall

This book is printed on acid-free paper

Contents

Introduction

In my previous work on the haunted places of Scotland, *Scottish Ghosts*, I noted that Scotland was a land of many ghosts and spirits. The book then went on to give details of over 250 hauntings throughout the length and breadth of the country. At the time I thought that I had covered most of the haunted locations that existed, but here is a second volume of spirits and spectres, with a further 200 cases of strange happenings all over the land. Readers of the previous book will be delighted to know that there is no duplication in the present volume — all the examples given are new.

Scottish Ghosts naturally included all the most famous examples of haunted buildings, from Glamis Castle to Edinburgh, but the reader will find many other interesting examples in the following pages. There are tales of ghosts appearing in many other castles and tower houses, as well as hauntings taking place in country houses. Old inns and pubs are favourite residences of spirits of a paranormal kind, and herein are numerous examples. Town hotels are often haunted also,

1

and examples from all over the country are given.

Poltergeist activity is less common than the sighting of a ghost, but is usually more frightening in that the witness sees items moving around the room. In a number of circumstances these can be extremely violent instances, with victims suffering nightmares from what they have experienced. This inexplicable movement of solid objects is often put down to some form of poltergeist.

Ghosts do not necessarily appear in ancient places. Very often the spectre is witnessed in modern homes. In many of these examples the spirit that appears is dressed in clothing from an earlier period, suggesting that perhaps the house occupies the site of an earlier building. Why the ghost appears is the subject of much speculation: is it to warn off the current resident, or perhaps it is searching for something, or someone, left behind?

A good number of ghosts can be identified as persons who lived in earlier decades, or even centuries. In many cases the witness has later identified whom they saw by reference to old photographs, or in the case of older examples, from oil portraits. Usually the person who spotted the ghost has not seen the painting or picture before, so they cannot be accused of some form of subliminal memory retention.

The author has spoken to many people who have seen ghosts over the years. Most of these people are genuine and are in no way freaks of any kind. They are quite adamant that they did see something that cannot be explained by any other means, and in most cases what they saw did not frighten them in any way. In fact, in most cases of ghosts being sighted, as soon as they are noticed or 'become aware' of the human presence, they tend to disappear rather suddenly.

Ghosts seem to manifest in front of certain members of the population who are receptive to their presence. These people tend to see ghosts everywhere, and mediums or other psychic people often claim to be able to explain hauntings to those who live in a haunted building. Other folk only ever witness one ghost in their lifetime, perhaps in their youth, though the experience can happen at any time and anywhere. The vast majority of the population however (the author included) have never seen a ghost, and look on the whole psychic world as something that may or may not exist. It is only when we someday might experience our own haunting that we will fully accept their existence.

How to explain the sighting of a ghost is still much of a mystery, and no doubt will be for many years. Different suggestions have been made, from them 'living' in a different temperature zone to the rest of us (hence the cold feeling often experienced when they are present), to the claim that they are like photographic replays that were the result of a massive outgoing of energy at one time, such as a murder. The latter theory is harder to explain when the ghost is of someone who died in uneventful circumstances, or even if the person is still alive, as is the case in 'time slips'.

Hauntings have been divided into different categories. Presences are those spectres that just appear in the same place on a regular basis. In many cases there may not even be a sighting, just the fact that the witness feels uncomfortable and cannot explain what the problem is. Replay ghosts are those which appear and seem to re-enact events from the past. Time slips are when someone appears in a different time zone. These cases may often be of someone who is still alive, and yet someone sees them, perhaps many miles away. Interactive spirits are those who appear to someone and converse or respond as though they were human, yet at a later time the witness discovers that this was impossible, or else the spirit disappears in front of their eyes after some time has lapsed. Poltergeists have already been mentioned. These are associated with solid objects being moved. In a number of cases poltergeist activity is associated with an individual person, rather than a place.

This book is full of spectres of all sorts. In some cases only the bare facts are known, such as a certain building or room therein is supposed to be haunted. Perhaps someone many years ago saw something that could not readily be explained. In other cases more detail can be furnished, especially when the building is still subject to sightings from more than one person.

I hope that the reader enjoys this collection of spectres and other hauntings — I certainly enjoyed compiling it!

Dane Love
Auchinleck, 2001

1

White Ladies

This classic ghost appears as a female figure, dressed in white, in buildings ranging from ancient castles to country houses. Hundreds of them are reported annually, and millions of sightings have been made over the centuries. These 'White Ladies' are usually sad or despondent figures wandering the corridors of ancient dwellings, seemingly searching for something, or someone, which will allow their spirit to eventually find the peace it longs for.

Some of the White Ladies are claimed to be the spirits of known women from the past — others are totally obscure, a supernatural reminder of something that happened in the building's history. The 'White Lady of the Biel' is one of the former. She is thought to be the wandering spirit of Anne Bruce, wife of the 3rd Lord Belhaven. Most sightings of her spirit are experienced in 'The Lady's Walk', which passes through the grounds around the mansion, though one or two have been made within the old house itself.

The Biel is a rather grand old Gothic

castellated mansion that incorporates a fourteenth century castle within it. The Hamiltons owned it for many years, Sir John Hamilton of Broomhouse being raised to the peerage with the title Lord Belhaven and Stenton in 1647. The 2nd Lord, John Hamilton, opposed the succession of James VII and campaigned against the Union of Parliaments in 1707. He was imprisoned for his beliefs, and died in 1708. John Hamilton succeeded as the 3rd Lord Belhaven. He married Anne Bruce, a daughter of Andrew Bruce of Earlshall Castle in Fife. Her grandfather, Sir Andrew Bruce, was an infamous persecutor of the Covenanters, responsible for slaying dozens of men for their religious beliefs.

Lord Belhaven was a representative peer of Scotland in 1715. He was appointed Governor of Barbados but was never to reach his post. The ship that was to take him there left the English mainland but foundered on the rocks off the Scilly Isles on 17 November 1721. All those on board the vessel were lost at sea.

Lady Belhaven discovered that her husband had been unfaithful to her, and she went into a sulk that lasted for many months. Although she was a very beautiful woman, and the desire of many a man, she spurned any advances, preferring instead to wander through the grounds of The Biel. Whilst still alive she received the epithet 'The White Lady' because of her very pale complexion, and it was said that when she drank claret the red colour could be seen through the skin of her throat. When Anne died her spirit remained restless, flitting among the trees lining the drives of the grounds, its forlorn appearance manifesting before the unwary traveller.

The White Lady at Castle Levan was also mistreated by her husband. The ghost does not seem to make a regular appearance, but throughout the history of the castle has frightened one or two unsuspecting visitors. The castle was for many years ruinous, the roof having been removed and the interior stripped, but in recent years the tower house was restored and occupied once more. Today Castle Levan is not your average Scottish castle, for its grounds have been developed as a housing estate, in the midst of which the sandstone tower looks rather incongruous.

Levan's White Lady is thought to be the spirit of Lady Marion Montgomerie. She was renowned for her contempt of the tenants and residents on the estate, not being averse to mistreating and torturing them herself. Lady Montgomerie was convicted and sentenced to death by Mary of Guise, the mother of Mary Queen of Scots. However, probably as she was a woman, this sentence was reduced to being placed under house arrest. When her husband returned from service in the army and found out what his wife had been up to in his absence he was furious. He locked her up in one of the castle's rooms and left her there for a number of weeks. Lady Montgomerie cried with pain as the days passed, for her husband refused to give her any food. At length she died, leaving her mournful spirit to wander through the castle.

Some folk claim that the White Lady of Castle Levan has never existed. They say that she was created in the imagination of a Semple-Stewart son in order to persuade his parents that the old castle had become too old-fashioned and cramped for his aspirations. As a result a new mansion named Castle Levan (or Levanne) was erected nearby in the Georgian style early in the nineteenth century.

The White Lady that haunts Dalmahoy House at Ratho in Midlothian is thought to be the apparition of Lady Mary Douglas, daughter of the Earl of Morton. Those folk who have seen this friendly spectre have often commented on the likeness of the spirit with the face of Lady Mary, whose portrait hangs on the walls. She married George Watson (d. 1723), founder of George Watson's School in Edinburgh. The Dalmahoys of that ilk built the mansion around 1710. It was sold in 1720 to the Dalrymples and in 1760 was acquired by the Douglases. Today it is a rather grand country house hotel, complete with country club and golf courses.

Lady Mary's spirit has appeared in the old part of the house, wandering from room to room. She has been seen in a number of the original bedrooms, as well as in the corridors, but her feint appearance is so calm and peaceful that it leaves the witness unperturbed.

The White Lady of Edzell Castle in Angus is not so pleasant. The spirit, which has been witnessed many times over the centuries, seems to have a rather pungent and unpleasant odour. Even in recent times, more than four hundred years after her death, the smell is still apparent, and seems not to have faded with time. Historic Scotland (an agency responsible for safeguarding the nation's built heritage) now protects the castle, and the gardens are one of its main features.

The tale of Edzell's White Lady is a rather tragic one. The earthly personage that the ghost formerly had was that of Catherine Campbell, second wife of David Lindsay, 9th Earl of Crawford, who had died in 1558. Catherine 'died' twenty years later and was placed in the family burial vault. 'Died' is in inverted commas, for in fact she had only fallen into a coma for some reason or other, and was actually very much alive. Nevertheless, her grieving family had her body laid out in the coffin and this was placed in the vault at Edzell church.

The parish sexton saw the body of Lady Lindsay as she was laid out in her coffin, and noticed her rather fine, and no doubt expensive, wedding ring. Later that night, in the hours of darkness, he stole into the kirkyard and forced his way into the Lindsay vault. He lifted the lid from the coffin and tried to remove the ring from the lady's finger, but found that her finger was swollen and he was unable to remove it. With his pocket knife held in trembling hands, and a bounding heart, he hacked at the finger to try and cut it off, and thereby steal the ring.

Catherine, however, only being in a coma, was disturbed by the pain of her finger being sliced in the darkness. The sexton was terrified when the corpse seemingly came to life, and shot off out of the vault as fast as he was able. Lady Lindsay rose from the coffin and stumbled from the vault out into the darkness. It took her some time to realize where she was, but once she got her bearings she headed off in the direction of the castle. The night was cold, and she was still weak, having eaten nothing for days. Although she reached the gateway to the castle, she was too weak to waken the sleeping residents and she succumbed to exposure. The next morning her family found her corpse outside the castle gate, but she really was dead this time and was put back into the vault.

Reports of a white apparition both at the old churchyard and at Edzell's ruins have been reported over the years. Many of the sightings have taken place in the rather attractive formal garden that lies in front of the ruins, and psychic investigators have often reported that as soon as they open the gate into the garden, or pass through the corner summer-house, they are instantly overcome by a feeling of something being present. Historic Scotland staff have witnessed her fleeting image and describe her as being dressed in ancient-styled floral clothing.

Between Falkirk and Cumbernauld is the ancient tower house known as Castle Cary. The oldest part is a tower erected in 1485, to which a wing was added in the seventeenth century. Although built by the Livingstons, the Baillie family owned the castle for some time. A distant cousin, General William Baillie of Letham, was a noted Covenanter. He was a natural child of Sir William Baillie of Lamington. Active in the European wars under Gustavus Adolphus, he later fought against the Royalists at the battles of Alford and Kilsyth in 1645 where the soldiers under the Marquis of Montrose defeated the Covenanters on both occasions. After the defeat at Kilsyth, Baillie rested for a while at Castle Cary, after which the Royalists burned the tower. When Baillie died is not known, but his ghost has been reported at Castle Cary.

It is said that Baillie's spirit returned there out of remorse for the troubles he caused the family and their tower in his life. It has been claimed that he is trying to help put matters right once again. The ghost of General Baillie is said to be a rather noisy spirit, and most of the strange noises heard in and around the castle are attributed to him. A few folk have seen the ghost of Baillie. Most sightings are made from the garden. Visitors have looked up at the tower and seen his figure looking back down at them from an upper window. From the position his head takes at the window it has been surmised that Baillie was a rather short man, and the ghost is often described as 'The Wee Man of Castle Cary' as a result.

Castle Cary is also home to a White Lady. One of the lairds had a daughter known as Elizabeth, or Lizzie. Her father doted on her, and as she was a very beautiful woman he had high hopes of a grand marriage, perhaps to a duke or earl. He introduced a number of suitable suitors to her, but she seemed to dislike all of them. At length her father became rather suspicious, and sent her off to live with some relatives by the side of Loch Lomond.

Lizzie returned to Castle Cary some weeks later. Suddenly she seemed to have an interest in writing letters to her cousins. These were frequent and quickly replied to. Her father became inquisitive of their contents, and intercepted one before his daughter received it. He discovered that she had fallen in love with a young laird from the Lennox. He was the proprietor of just a few acres, and worse still, his surname was Graham. It was the Grahams under Montrose who had been responsible for setting the castle alight during the years of persecution.

Baillie was so angry that he ripped up the letter and sent for his daughter. She did not deny her love for her boyfriend, causing his rage to inflame even more. He forbade her from seeing him again, but the young lovers often found ways around this. Sometimes they met secretly in Castlecary Glen, but in time Lizzie's father found out. He took his daughter up to the uppermost garret in the old tower where he locked her up. Feeding her only on bread and water, he intended keeping her there until such time as she saw sense.

Lizzie was not to be beat, however. She had a faithful servant and she managed to tell her about her lover. A message was sent to Graham and he arrived at Castle Cary one night with friends. He could not make any attempt at breaking into the castle, but he knew in which room his girlfriend was held. After throwing stones at the window to attract her attention, he asked his friends to take a plaid and hold it tight, creating a landing sheet. Lizzie climbed on to the parapet of the castle and jumped over the edge. She fell four storeys down to the sheet where she was safely caught. Lizzie and the Graham then stole away into the night.

Far away from Castle Cary, Lizzie and her man were married. Although they lived happily for a while, word reached her that her father was dead. It turns out that he was so upset with the eloping daughter that he suffered a stroke and died. Although Lizzie

16

had defied her father, she still loved him very much. That he died as a result of her actions caused her to worry so much that she died prematurely. Her spirit returned to Castle Cary where it manifested thereafter as a White Lady.

The ghost of Lizzie has been reported in various parts of the castle. Most sitings, however, seem to have taken place on the principal stairway. As one walks down the steps the feeling of someone following you is often experienced. It is as if the spirit of Lizzie is wandering through the castle searching for her father.

There are a number of White Ladies that have been reported in the old kingdom of Fife. One of these, the White Lady of Falkland Palace, glides along the Tapestry Gallery. Little is known of who she was in life, but a number of sightings have been made of her here. Some actually describe her as the 'Grey Lady' and on one occasion a seasonal cleaner witnessed her gliding down the length of the Gallery before disappearing through the wall at a spot where there was formerly a doorway.

Little is known about the White Lady of Kilmany also. A quiet spot near Kilmany Cottage, which lies on the edge of Kilmany village, is known as the Ghouls' Den. It is claimed that a White Lady haunts this ravine and is sometimes joined by other spectres.

South of Kilmany, between St Andrews and Cupar, is the little village of Kemback. It is located at the foot of another ravine known as Dura Den. During the years of persecution, when the Covenanters were forced to flee their homes to preserve their lives, this den was a popular hiding place. One of those who sought refuge here was a member of the Schivas family. He was the laird of Kemback House, but had to leave his home and live rough in a cave that can still be seen here. Schivas' wife would leave the house and walk during the hours of sunset to the cave with food for him. One night, however, the redcoats caught her as she made her way into the den. She steadfastly refused to reveal where her husband was hiding. So determined was she that she would keep the secret, the soldiers decided to hang her. They forced her down the roadway to Dairsie Bridge. Using a rope she was hanged over the parapet until her body was left lifeless. Since that time a White Lady apparition has been reported in the vicinity of the bridge, den and Kemback House. A room in the old mansion (which was extended in the baronial style in 1907) is still known as the White Lady's Room.

In Kirkcaldy is the Kingswood Hotel, located on Kinghorn Road. Many years ago, when the building was a private house, a young girl named Patsy Jean Fagan lived there with her parents, an uncle and a grandmother. She was only four years old at the time, but she often sensed the presence of a ghostly spirit. The family named this spectre 'Jenny', but it seemed to pick on young Patsy. On many occasions the girl felt a pinch on her bottom, and nothing was visible to explain why this was so. The nearest thing the family could imagine the ghost to be was a goose, for it would chase the girl round the room, pecking her. The girl also witnessed a White Lady one day when she was in the grounds of the house. Patsy was in a distressed state at the time, but turned round when she thought she saw someone behind her. What she saw then will never leave her memory. A woman stood there, draped in a magnificent flowing dress. The material was thin and delicate, and formed itself over the lady's flowing curves. As she gazed at the ghost Patsy found herself calming down, and some inner warmth passing through her body. Suddenly she heard voices, and recognized them as coming from her father. She turned round to see him, but when she turned back discovered that the White Lady had gone.

Kilbryde Castle stands to the north of Dunblane. It is a rather fine building that is still inhabited. One day a gamekeeper surnamed MacGregor was in the castle courtyard when he heard a noise from an upstairs window. When he looked up he saw the face of a female looking back down at him. He did not recognize who the person was, but was very concerned because he knew that the castle was supposed to be unoccupied. He quickly gathered together the assistance of the estate gardeners and, with his gun for protection, made a thorough search through the building. Nothing was found, and the room from where the face had looked at him was totally undisturbed.

The gamekeeper had probably witnessed the White Lady of Kilbryde. An old blacksmith on the estate regularly witnessed this spirit near to the old chapel. Each time he tried to talk to her the manifestation slowly disappeared. Who the White Lady was is unknown, but it is said that there is a part in the castle where three strange steps lead up to a former doorway. Beyond the doorway has long since been demolished in castle reconstruction work, leaving the three steps to nowhere. In the passage leading to it were bloodstains on the floor and tradition claims that a woman was murdered here.

A second murder in the vicinity of the castle resulted in a second ghost. It is said that Sir Malise Graham of Kilbryde fell in love with Lady Anne Chisholm, who lived at nearby Cromlix Castle. They often met at a romantic grove in Kilbryde Glen, but after some time Sir Malise (who became known as the 'Black Knight of Kilbryde') began to tire of his sweetheart. He took things to the extreme, and resorted to murder. Lady Anne was killed at the spot where they usually met, and her corpse was buried beneath the soil by the side of the stream. The family searched but could not find where she had gone, for no foul deed had been suspected.

Within days there were tales of a ghost haunting the policies of the castle. Those who had seen it described the spectre as having long white robes tainted with blood. She often appeared to residents at the castle and she seemed to be beckoning them to come to her. No one who saw her was willing to accede.

Sir Malise Graham was killed in battle and the property passed to another. The new owner was well aware of the ghost, but had never seen her. One night, shortly after inheriting, he was wandering round the garden when he spotted the figure of a woman standing near to the gate. He was not thinking of the spectre at the time, and went to see whom the lady was. As he approached he noticed the bloodstained dress, and his throat dried when he realized what he was seeing. The lady directed him to follow, and so enchanted by her was he that he followed her to Kilbryde Glen. At a lonely spot she seemed to signal to him and then disappeared.

The next day the new laird returned to the glen, armed with a spade. He dug at the spot where the spirit had disappeared, and after a few spades of earth were dug he soon found the body of Lady Anne. Her corpse was taken away and buried in the estate cemetery, after which her ghost was never seen again.

Near to Balmyre farm, in the Angus parish of Kilspindie, is a spot known as the Lady's Brig. This is located about halfway up the Smithy Brae, which leads from Kilspindie Church to Balmyre, where the road makes a particularly sharp turn to cross a stream. The spirit of a White Lady was in past years reported here, but of the ghost's history no one seems to know anything. Lawrence Melville, in *The Fair Land of Gowrie*, speculates that the spirit may be that of a woman who had been murdered nearby, her corpse not being very well buried, causing her to roam the district. Another option he considers was that she was a murderess herself, and following her own death rested none-too-peacefully in the grave. A third option was that she was the apparition of a 'good white-veiled nun', back to visit the sylvan scene of her earthly labours.

Those who have witnessed the White Lady of Evelick, as Melville styles her, state that her image passed down the Smithy Brae, taking the side which was in the shadow of the trees. On her way back up the glen she seems to have preferred the other side, openly appearing in the silvery moonlight. Whether or not the spirit had anything to do with Evelick Castle, the ruins of which are located farther up the hill than Balmyre, is not known.

Not far from Kilspindie, at the opposite end of the Carse of Gowrie, is Castle Huntly, which for many years operated as one of Her Majesty's Borstal institutions. The original tower dates from the middle of the fifteenth century, but the castle has been altered and extended on a number of occasions. The Earl of Strathmore, who also owned (and still does) Glamis Castle, which is located fifteen miles to the north, at one time owned Castle Huntly. Tradition claims that there was an underground tunnel linking the two castles, but this is even more suspect than the many supposed tunnels that are claimed to connect closer buildings.

Castle Huntly's White Lady has been reported down through the centuries. She is said to have been a daughter of the Lyon of Strathmore family who became over-familiar with one of the male servants on the estate. Her family regarded her crime as heinous, and she was locked up in a small room in one of the castle's upper floors. This room was later named the Waterloo Room, after a Colonel Paterson who arrived at the castle with news of Wellington's victory. The window in the room was one hundred feet above the level of the courtyard, but the daughter tried to make an escape from it, only to lose her grip in the process and plummet to her death on the cobbled yard below. Other accounts of the spirit claim that the daughter was not trying to escape, but that someone in the family pushed her from the window, murdering both the daughter and her unborn love-child. The window from which the girl fell was long pointed out by the locals.

The White Lady not only haunted the Waterloo Room: she has been witnessed in various parts of the parkland surrounding the castle. There is one particular spot in the castle grounds where the spirit manifested so often that a bridge there became known as the Bogle Bridge. Residents of the Carse of Gowrie who were travelling at night would make a detour to avoid the bridge rather then cross it in the dark. One April afternoon, when the sky was black and thunder was approaching, a man walking along one of the castle drives witnessed the spirit flitting among the trees, the apparition appearing as it passed from behind one tree to another. The man was not scared of what he saw, for he had long heard of the ghost in tales handed down through his family, but this was his first time in witnessing it.

A maid in the castle told of how she was always nervous whenever she had to enter the haunted chamber. She also related that English servants employed in the castle at various times had been scared by what they experienced in the room. On one occasion two young ladies from the district were dared into spending the night in the haunted room. All went well for a while until the midnight chimes were heard resounding through the castle. From then on the atmosphere in the room was such that the ladies were forced to vacate the apartment and spend the night elsewhere.

Historic Scotland protects Balvenie Castle in Banffshire. It is a rather grand ruin, standing on a low hill on the edge of the village of Dufftown. The castle is home to a White Lady that has been witnessed irregularly over the years. A visitor saw another apparition in 1994, although no one else seems to have witnessed the same scene at any other time. The witness experienced the sight of two horses, along with a groom. Other spectral happenings were also seen, though these failed to materialize into anything recognizable.

Carbisdale Castle is one of the finest, yet most recent, of the castle-style country houses to be erected in Scotland. Its tale is one of unhappy families, for the dowager Duchess of Sutherland erected the house in 1910. She had married the third Duke as his second wife but the rest of his family hated her. When he died in 1892 she was left a considerable fortune. The new duke refused to allow her to live on the estate, and would not allow her some ground on which to build herself a home. As a result, she bought a piece of ground just over the border in Ross-shire and there built the massive and impressive castle with its dramatic tower, so large that the new duke would see it every time he passed on the road to Dunrobin.

Even though it is a comparatively modern building, the spirit of a White Lady haunts the castle, which is now operated by the Scottish Youth Hostels Association. She has appeared to guests at various times over the years, but no one is ever really scared when they see her. Reports of her visits have been made in various rooms throughout the extensive building. Most folk think that the ghost is the manifestation of the Duchess Blair, as she is known from her maiden name.

The Hunter's Tryst Inn, which stands in Edinburgh's Oxgangs Road, has its own White Lady. The inn was erected as a coaching halt in the eighteenth century to serve passengers on the road that linked Dalkeith with the west, bypassing the city centre. In some of the rooms the White Lady has appeared to guests, but who she was in life is unknown.

Near the Aberdeenshire village of Oldmeldrum is Meldrum House, at the centre of which is a castle c. 1236 to which various additions have been made. The house had been in the same family for generations, though it passed through the female line on occasions, until fairly recently. It is now a country house hotel. For many years there have been tales of the building being haunted by a White Lady that originally seemed only to appear to young children. Many infants who had been left alone in their rooms or nurseries would tell their parents that a nice lady in a long white dress had appeared. She would play with and look after the children for a time, but would always disappear before any adult returned.

That the ghost only appeared to youngsters was long accepted, but in 1985 an adult male was awakened during the night by the feeling of her kissing him on the face. The kiss was extremely cold, and it may be significant that it took place during a fierce thunderstorm, when the rain was battering against the windows of the building. On another occasion a guest in the haunted room felt that an unseen force was pushing him into the mattress of his bed. This force seemed to last for a minute or so. The husband of the owner of Meldrum House also made a sighting of the ghost walking in an upstairs corridor. A portrait of the human likeness of the White Lady hangs on a wall of Meldrum House.

Another Aberdeenshire mansion that is home to a White Lady is Ardoe House, now also a country house hotel. Located on the southern Deeside road, the mansion is a typically Scots-baronial confection. Alexander Milne Ogston had purchased the estate for £19,000 in 1839 but it was his son who erected the present house in 1878. The spirit is said to have transferred from the original building that formerly occupied the site. One tale claims that the manifestation is that of Katherine Ogston, wife of Alexander Milne Ogston, a successful manufacturer of soap. What happened to Mrs Ogston to cause her to haunt the building is not known, for there seems to be no gruesome tale connected with her. A portrait of Mrs Ogston still hangs on the main staircase of the hotel. Witnesses who have seen the spirit include the entertainer Tommy Steele, who stayed at the hotel in 1958. One of the more recent sightings took place in 1990. The witness saw the ghost on the principal staircase. He thought at first that it was a woman sleepwalking, and he was able to watch her make her way to the main doorway, where the figure promptly disappeared.

A second tale is associated with Ardoe's White Lady. According to the local gossips, a daughter of the family was subjected to a brutal rape at the hands of a local man. She found herself pregnant, and in despair decided to kill herself and the unborn child in order to prevent any shame on both her and her family. This tale is certainly more sinister than the link with Mrs Ogston!

2

Inns and Spirits

The traditional Scottish inn dates only from the eighteenth century, when travel became more common and roads were improved. Landowners erected inns on their estates as a means of attracting custom to their area, and in many instances they were also marks of his prestige. Travellers frequented the inns, and victualling and stabling were available for their horses. Prior to this it was the custom in Scotland for travellers, of whom there were few, to invite themselves in to almost anyone's home, where they would be looked after in the customary manner.

It is claimed that many of the older inns in Scotland are haunted, and our tour of these will commence at Gretna, the village that most travellers pass on the route north when arriving in Scotland by road. West of Gretna, Dumfries and Galloway stretches towards Stranraer and Wigtownshire, an area often bypassed by the tourist who tends to rush northward to Edinburgh or the Highlands. Dumfries is a provincial town, nicknamed

'Queen of the South'. It has many connections with the poet Robert Burns, who spent
his final few years here, and whose grave is
located in St Michael's churchyard.

In Dumfries is the Globe Inn, where Burns
himself is known to have enjoyed a drink.
Here he met Anna (or Helen) Park, who was
a barmaid. Burns had a bit of a reputation for
loving the lassies, and Anna fell under his
spell. She was later to present him with a
daughter, Elizabeth, only nine days before his
wife gave birth to another of his children,
William, in 1791. Anna appears to have died
shortly after the birth, and Burns' wife
brought up the child. She seems to have been
accommodating as far as Burns' affairs were
concerned, and was reported as having stated
that 'Oor Robbie should ha'e had twa wives!'
The barmaid was celebrated in the poet's
'Yestreen I had a pint o' wine'. She lived in an
upstairs room at the inn, and here the spirit
of a woman has been witnessed over the
years.

The Globe Inn dates from 1610 and stands
in the High Street. It has had a reputation for
many years of being haunted by Anna Park.
Regulars at the bar tell their tales of the
strange spirit, and guests who have spent the
night in the room where Anna lived in the
eighteenth century have awakened to noises

that they were unable to explain.

One of the most recent sightings of Anna Park took place in 1996. Kirsty Mawhinney had been passing along a corridor when she caught sight of something out of the corner of her eye. When she turned round she was amazed to see the figure of a woman making her way up a staircase at speed. The apparition was dressed in an old-fashioned full-skirted dress and probably remained in Mrs Mawhinney's sight for just a few seconds. She was so shocked that she had to return to the kitchen where she stood shaking. Other employees returned with Mrs Mawhinney to the spot where she saw the spirit, but by this time the figure of Anna was long gone.

West of Dumfries is the village of Crocketford, where the Galloway Inn stands by the roadside. The hotel dates from 1856 but owes its origin to the Buchanites, who settled here. This religious sect comprised of adherents of Elizabeth Buchan (1738–91), who believed that she was the woman referred to in Revelations 12. This states:

There was a woman, whose dress was the sun and who had the moon under her feet and a crown of twelve stars on her head. She was soon to give birth, and the pains and suffering of childbirth made her cry out . . . [A huge red dragon] stood in front of the woman, in order to eat her child as soon as it was born. Then she gave birth to a son, who will rule over all nations with an iron rod. But the child was snatched away and taken to God and his throne. The woman fled to the desert, to a place God had prepared for her, where she will be taken care of for 1,260 days.

Elizabeth Buchan managed to persuade others that she had heavenly powers, and they joined her at a convent at Crocketford, now the Galloway Arms. The ghost of Elizabeth Buchan is believed to haunt the building to this day, and according to the locals she appears at irregular intervals.

Almost due south of Crocketford, the road round the coast arrives at the small village of Auchencairn. Here is the Smugglers' Inn, a traditional whitewashed inn in the Scots style. This is home to a spirit that the regulars have nicknamed 'Old Gladys'. This spirit has even manifested on film. On one occasion Border Television was filming at the inn. The takes were all completed, but when the film was later played a very faint figure appeared on the screen. No one was aware of seeing the spirit whilst the cameras were rolling.

Old Gladys has a reputation for moving things around. There are many tales of objects mysteriously moving from one place to another when no one is present. Even scarier are the cases when objects move in full view of guests at the inn. During a dinner party held at the inn a powder compact levitated out of an open handbag that was sitting on the floor. Gladys is also particular about who sits on her favourite chair, which is located by the side of the fire. Should anyone she apparently dislikes decide to rest there, she has been known to make her displeasure apparent to the culprit.

There used to be an old inn at Dalleagles in Ayrshire. This clachan is located on the roadway that links New Cumnock with Dalmellington. The inn was formerly a private house, but has long since gone. Writing in 1899, Helen Steven relates the story behind the haunting:

A tale was told of a landlord who was murdered by a band of Englishmen who came to work at the lead mines. From an upper room there was a ladder leading to a loft. In that room a servant girl was sleeping one night, when suddenly the stillness was broken by a horrible noise, as if a body, or some heavy article like a sack of corn, was being dragged down the ladder. Rudely awakened, the girl in her terror could neither move nor speak. When she came to herself she flew down to the kitchen, where the other members of the household were in bed, and told her tale. But they had been aroused by the same dreadful sound, and consternation seized the whole family. Next day the news spread, and some believed and others smiled sceptically, and a young man of strong nerves declared he would put the truth of the story to the test. When night came once more, this man quietly ascended to the room, accompanied by his faithful collie. The loft and ladder were carefully examined, but nothing of a suspicious character could be seen. Whistling softly to himself, perhaps to keep up his courage, he lay down upon the bed. The peculiar circumstances under which he found himself kept him awake long after his lowly companion was chasing his natural enemies through dream-land. Just as midnight struck, the dog awoke, howled dreadfully, and with one bound sprang into the bed and down beside his master. And then that horrible noise was again heard throughout the room. First of all the trap was lifted, and with a crash and a thud a heavy body fell to the floor.

Cumnock in Ayrshire is home to an old inn formerly known as the Tup Inn, but presently named Jenny Tear's after a former proprietress, Janet Tear. The building has been altered over the years, but at one time there was an apartment located over the front lounge. On a number of occasions in the 1970s the proprietor at that time heard the sound of feet walking about in the room over the lounge. On investigation he found nothing to account for the sound, and eventually came to accept some spirit or other perhaps made the noise. As a maid formerly occupied the room it was assumed that the ghost might be that of a young girl who worked in the building, but from what period the ghost dates is not known.

The island of Arran lies in the Firth of Clyde to the west of Ayrshire. At the southern end of the island is the tiny village of Lagg, where the Lagg Inn was erected as a coaching establishment in the eighteenth century. The inn has been expanded considerably since that time, and now is celebrated for its fine food. The building has a reputation for being haunted by a local laird who sold his soul to the devil. Tradition claims that he was so strapped for cash that he made a pact with the 'Earl of Hell' and agreed that he could claim his soul on his death in return for sufficient funds to clear his debts.

In Glasgow is Graham's Bar, located in the Saltmarket, one of the oldest streets in the city. This pub is a typical Glasgow local, with a spartan bar and cosy lounge. The apparition of an old woman wearing a shawl over her head has been witnessed a number of times by staff employed in the bar, and regulars claim that she has appeared for many years. Who the old woman may have been in her earthly life is unknown, but it has been speculated that she lived in a house on this site.

The tiny village of Ardentinny sits on Loch Long in Argyll. It is something of a backwater, but was an important crossing point in the days when drovers brought cattle from the western highlands to the lowland markets. The Ardentinny Hotel dates from around 1720 and was built as a refreshment point for drovers on the march. Some folk, however, claim that the hotel is at least four hundred years old, and that Mary Queen of Scots rested here awhile in 1563, *en route* to Inveraray.

The Ardentinny Inn has some rather unusual spirits living there. These take the form of young children, and are usually only witnessed in one particular bedroom. Guests in the hotel have woken during the night to the sound of children in the apartment, thinking that some have managed to enter their room. However, the figures seem to disappear after a short while.

North of Argyll, in the country of Inverness, a number of other drovers' inns survive. Today these are more frequented by travellers and sportsmen. The Glenfinnan Inn is located at the head of Loch Shiel, on the road west from Fort William to Mallaig. It is said that the inn dates from 1658, but it has been extended and renamed over its life, and today is known as the Prince's House, after Bonnie Prince Charlie who may have sampled its hospitality. The inn boasts two ghosts, but the proprietors insist that they will not cause you any harm. One of the spirits is a Grey Lady, who flits along the corridors before disappearing. The other revenant is simply known as the Bearded Highlander, for it appears as a highland soldier. Whether or not this spirit was one of Bonnie Prince Charlie's followers, perhaps killed in one of the Jacobite battles, is unknown.

A few miles further west of Glenfinnan, still on the road to Mallaig, is the clachan of Lochailort. The Lochailort Inn suffered a fire in 1994, which seems to have brought all hauntings to an end, but prior to this two spirits had been witnessed at the inn. Before rebuilding, the old inn dated from around 1650, and like the Glenfinnan Inn was an important rest for drovers. Regulars and staff frequently witnessed the spirit of a woman. She wore a long blue dress and appeared from time to time. Other paranormal happenings at the inn included the sound of bagpipes being played. These are sometimes also experienced in the glen towards Loch Eilt, and tradition claims that the sound comes from the ghost of a soldier of the Jacobite rising.

On the island of Skye, which is part of Inverness-shire, stands the Broadford Hotel. This is an old two-and-a-half storey building, with the traditional Scots corbie-stepped gables, located on the edge of the village. The hotel seems to have a number of spirits resting there, and various reports describe different sights. Some guests at the hotel have reported what they describe as 'mists' appearing in the rooms. These often appear as an indeterminate shape, whereas others claim that they take the form of the human figure. Others do not see anything, but have suddenly become aware of a cold shiver running through their body, as if some presence is enfolding them. Poltergeist activity has also taken place, for over the years reports have been made of ladders and lamps moving of their own accord.

When the spirits at Broadford manifest into something more visible than just mist, they seem to take the form of a female figure. She has been witnessed making her way up the stairs, and also in the bar, where she seems to have a favourite chair. The spirit is said to belong to a former housekeeper at the hotel, but who she was and from what period is not known.

In the Moray town of Elgin is the Thunderton House, which now operates as a public house. The building incorporates a fourteenth century castle that was the town residence of the Earls of Moray. In the eighteenth century Lady Arradoul, a keen supporter of the Jacobite movement, occupied the house. When Bonnie Prince Charlie was marching towards his ultimate defeat at the Battle of Culloden, he stayed eleven nights here. It is said by some that it is his spirit that occupies the building. The faint sound of bagpipes being played has been heard in the inn, as well as inexplicable voices coming from the second floor. On a few occasions objects have seemingly moved by themselves. Other people claim that the spirit at Thunderton House is female in form, and that it is the manifestation of Lady Arradoul herself. Sightings of the ghost are rare, so it has not been possible to determine whether the spirit is male or female, or whether in fact there is more than one ghost present.

The Newtongarry Inn in Aberdeenshire stands remotely on the road between Huntly and Inverurie, at the junction with the road that crosses Gartly Moor to Insch. It is no longer an inn, having long ago been converted into a house, but it still retains the name. Local tradition insists that the inn was haunted, but the present occupiers, the Thomson family, state that they have never witnessed anything which would set the hairs on the back of their necks on edge. Those who claim the inn to be haunted describe events that included crockery mysteriously rattling on the shelf, and weird noises that could never be explained. These seem to have stopped in recent years.

In Aberdeen itself is Cameron's Inn, located in Little Belmont Street, which lies off the main shopping street of the city — Union Street. Not a lot is known about the spirit that frequents this hostelry, but tradition claims that regulars at the inn have witnessed inexplicable happenings over the years. The inn itself was an old coaching inn that still retains much of its character. A decorator employed to paint the ceiling of the lounge bar was working alone in the inn when he heard some knocks from the room above him. The painter knew that the room was supposed to be empty, for he was the only person in the building. However, he knocked a couple of times on the ceiling in return, only to be startled when the 'ghost' returned the sound. Another incident took place when a cleaner felt a strangely cold presence.

A relatively modern bar in Aberdeen is the Cocked Hat pub. Originally erected in 1955, the public house was owned by John Walker, who died in 1959. The premises were passed on to others, but for some reason Mr Walker manifested in the bar on many occasions thereafter. On one occasion a waitress spotted a man in the bar after the pub had been closed and the regulars had gone home. The waitress went for her boss, but when they returned and tried to find what they thought was a trespasser no one could be found. The waitress described what she saw, and her boss recognized the description as being Mr Walker. He used to wear a long coat and a hat with an upturned brim.

Dunkeld in Perthshire was a very important centre in history. Here the Tay could be crossed by ferry, there was a cathedral, and it became an important staging post on the great road to Inverness. In the village is the Atholl Arms Hotel, an old coaching establishment. It was originally known as the Duke of Atholl's Arms Inn and dates from around 1790. One of the hotel's old parlour maids died here, and her spirit has been witnessed a number of times over the years. She has been nicknamed 'Chrissie' by the staff, and seems to make appearances at night, wandering the corridors as if carrying out her work.

The Bridgend House Hotel at Callander (also in Perthshire) has an unusual history. It is thought to date from the seventeenth century, though some folk claim it to be as old as the previous century. The inn was built on top of an ancient right of way from the bridge (and previously a ford) to The Meadows. The ghosts who have been seen at the inn seem to follow this old route, passing through the inn's walls and rooms as though they did not exist.

Another old inn is the Lion and Unicorn, which is located in the Perthshire village of Thornhill, which actually is located nearer Stirling. The inn (which was formerly known as the Commercial Hotel) was established in 1635 as a drover's inn. The proprietors describe the spirit that makes its home there as a 'kind and happy ghost'. She seems to be a rather shy spectre, for she only appears to single witnesses. Those who have managed to catch a glimpse of her state that she is dressed in green. The locals have named the spirit Annie.

South of Thornhill, in Strathendrick, is the village of Fintry, nestling in the valley between the Campsie and Fintry hills. The Fintry Inn has a spirit that has appeared at different times. The proprietors have no idea who her earthly being was, or in what period she lived, but as the inn was built in 1750 she probably dates from some time after then. A number of guests at the inn have reported the manifestation appearing in their bedrooms, but she seems not to frighten them too much.

The Blane Valley Inn lies in the village of Blanefield, north of Glasgow, but in the country of Stirling. The inn building dates from around 1700, when it was erected as the Netherton Inn, being located in what was at one time referred to as the village of Netherton. There has always been some form of inn or public house here, serving the public and locals. The panelled ground floor of the inn is home to a White Lady. Her spectre is sometimes seen, or more commonly sensed, in the bar area, which is located at the centre of the building. There were formerly stairs leading from the bar to an apartment on the first floor, but these stairs have long since been removed in alterations to the building. The White Lady is usually sensed in the vicinity of the foot of the stairs, as though she appears or disappears at the spot where the stairs entered the bar.

On the southern side of the Campsie Hills is the village of Lennoxtown. Here can be found the Campsie View Hotel. Norrie Smith at one time owned it and it is claimed that his spirit still frequents the building. On many occasions strange things have happened, like the juke box playing to itself in the morning, items being moved from one place to another when no one was present, and drinks being left on the table when the bar had been cleared for the night. The strange movements have been attributed to Smith because it was typical of his actions, and whilst still alive he often used to relate that, 'This place won't work without me'.

In the Fife village of Falkland is the Covenanter's Hotel. The spirit that appears here has been claimed to be that of Mary Queen of Scots, who lived for a time in nearby Falkland Palace. In any case, a female figure has been seen a number of times in the hotel bedrooms by guests over the years. There are also reports of objects 'flying' across one of the rooms in the hotel for no apparent reason.

In Edinburgh's Royal Mile stands Whistle Binkie's bar, one of the most haunted pubs in the city. The cellars of the bar are the home of a spirit known as 'The Watcher', who seems to appear on a regular basis. It has been speculated that this male ghost lived in the seventeenth century. In 1994 a witness was able to reproduce a drawing of the spirit, detailing his appearance and dated attire. The cellars of the pub are a regular stop on one of the city's many 'ghost walks', and a good number of tourists have experienced the spirit. Even if the visitors do not see the full ghost, a number have reported witnessing a form of 'mist' in the vaults below the bar.

The strange occurrences at Whistle Binkie's are not restricted to the cellars. On many occasions sounds have been heard of a nature that cannot be explained. On one occasion the bar staff were startled to discover that an orange was able to slice itself. More astonishing, however, is the regular stopping of the bar clocks at 4.15 a.m.

Another Edinburgh bar, known as PJ Lyle's, is supposed to be haunted by a former regular. Some of the staff at the bar have heard the sound of footsteps walking across the rooms over the bar. From the sounds experienced it has been calculated that the spirit must have walked through one of the dividing walls, and on inspection of the rooms above no one is ever found, leaving no explanation for the sound.

Heading south from Edinburgh, on the A68, is the village of Pathhead. By the roadside just before the village is the Stair Arms Inn, which is an old corbie-stepped coaching halt. Lord and Lady Stair built it when Telford constructed a bridge across the gorge. At some point in the inn's history one of the chambermaids committed suicide. The spirit of the young lass has frequented the inn ever since, though it has been remarked that she makes rather few appearances. Any sightings that do take place seem to be within the inn's restaurant.

There are a number of old haunted inns in the Scottish Borders. This was a turbulent frontier-land up until the Union of the Crowns in 1603, after which things settled down. Border reivers crossed the Cheviot Hills to make raids on English towns, returning with booty in the form of cattle and horses.

Heading south from Edinburgh on the road through Pathhead, we come to the small town of Lauder, nestling in the sylvan Lauderdale. The Eagle Inn dates back to the early 1800s as an inn, but before this it was previously a manse. The spirit that haunts the inn perhaps dates back to these times. It may be a restless man of the cloth, unhappy at the current use of his home.

At Melrose, the George and Abbotsford Hotel stands in the village's main square. It too has connections with religion, for it was erected in 1740 on the site of the original High Church of Melrose. The spirits at this hotel seem not to make any appearances. Instead, the sound of footsteps is heard from the ceilings of rooms five to nine. Many guests spending the night at the hotel have heard the steps in the rooms above, and have even complained to the manager about it. When it is explained to them that there are no rooms above, for these bedrooms are on the top floor, the guests become shaken and find the hairs on their necks rising.

At Innerleithen, further up the Tweed valley from Melrose, is the Traquair Arms. This old coaching inn dates from 1836 but has been extended since. In the older part of the hotel, and only there, is the home of a Grey Lady spirit. This manifestation has only ever been witnessed from the rear, and all who have seen her describe her as wearing a long grey dress on which is a large bustle. Her hair is tied up in a bun. Who this spirit was in life is not known, nor even from what period in the inn's history.

Many other inns are haunted, though the ghosts who appear do so irregularly and little is known about them. Examples are numerous, and include the Cross Keys Inn at Denholm, Hawick. Here a spirit, which has been named 'Harry', frequents the cellars. Its presence was confirmed when a clairvoyant paid the bar a visit.

3

Haunted Hotels

Ghosts and spirits seem to enjoy the hospitality offered at many of Scotland's hotels. The previous chapter detailed the ghosts that appear in the smaller hotels and inns, whereas this chapter will look at the ghosts that haunt the larger and country-house style hotels.

The Houston House Hotel has as its core an ancient Scots tower house, to which has been added a more modern extension. It is located in the countryside near Uphall in West Lothian. The older part of the hotel is claimed to be haunted, and various guests have reported strange occurrences over the years.

In 1994 Ian and Christine Cameron travelled the short distance from their home in Linlithgow to the hotel where they proposed spending a romantic weekend. They booked in and were shown to Room 22. Everything was going smoothly until the couple went to bed. During the night Ian got up to go to the toilet. Whilst he was away

Christine was aware of someone, or something, climbing on to the bed alongside her. Just before this happened she had become aware of the room turning extremely cold. As the invisible spectre made its way up the bed Christine tried to let out a scream, but no sound came from her mouth. The apparition reached the top of the bed where it pinned Christine down on to the mattress, preventing her from moving. Ian returned towards the bed, and though he too did not see anything, he was aware of the terror his wife was experiencing. However, the ghost seems to have disappeared just as quickly as it had appeared. The couple were unable to sleep after the experience and spent the rest of the night sitting up with the lights on. They checked out of the hotel the next morning and although they have been back since, they always make sure that they book into a different room.

In Aberdeen a female manifestation appears in the older part of the Amatola Hotel, which is located at 448 Great Western Road. Here is an example of the spirit being similar in appearance to a portrait that hangs in the hotel, in this case of the great-great-grandmother of the owners of the building. The facial expression of the spirit is similar to the painting, and those guests who have witnessed the ghost have described her as wearing clothing that would seem to date the spirit to having lived sometime in the nineteenth century. Even the folk who have not seen the portrait, or heard of its story, have described the ghost in a similar manner, and are surprised when the portrait is pointed out to them.

Guests at the Amatola who have seen the hotel's ghost usually witness it appearing on the landing of the stairs. Shortly after noticing the spirit, the figure seems to disappear.

The Norwood Hall Hotel stands in Garthdee Road, at Cults, to the west of Aberdeen. Norwood Hall was built as a house in 1887 for the Ogston family, who had made their fortune with the Pears' Soap company. The Ogstons were related to the Ogstons of Ardoe, mentioned in the first chapter. Some say that the house was actually built for a mistress of Colonel James Ogston. Ogston and his wife did not get on very well, and the two ghosts who are said to appear here are thought to be of the pair. James had a mistress, of whom his wife was aware, but no pleading could persuade him to give her up. In despair she died, and her restless soul has wandered the vicinity of the house ever since.

The apparition of James Ogston himself has also been reported, though why he would be unsettled and still haunt the building is unknown. Sightings of this spirit have been made in the dining-room of the hotel in recent years.

A murder is thought to have been the cause of death of a female who now haunts the Earls Court Hotel, which is also in Aberdeen. The hotel, which dates from the Victorian era and stands in Queens Road, is home to a manifestation that has been seen occasionally by guests. Of her history, little else is known.

The White Dove Hotel in Aberdeen no longer stands, having been demolished some years ago. At one time a guest named Miss Vining arrived but soon after checking in she was taken ill and confined to her bed. The hotel proprietors were aware of her illness and when she failed to improve sent for a doctor. He examined Miss Vining and pronounced that she seemed to be suffering from some form of tropical disease. He decided that the lady required constant medical attention, so he arranged for a nurse to wait by her bedside. The nurse spent most of her time checking her patient and making sure that she was comfortable. However, she was decidedly uneasy regarding the atmosphere in the room, which she could not explain. She reckoned that it must be something to do with the condition of her patient that was causing her to feel rather strange also.

Miss Vining fell asleep and the nurse sat by her bed on a chair. She was reading a book to pass the time. At one point she looked up and caught sight of a young girl sitting on the chair at the foot of the bed. The nurse got up to scold the child for coming into a sick woman's room, and to check whether she had her mother's permission to be there. As she got up the child held up her hand as if to warn her to come no nearer. Suddenly the nurse seemed to lose her powers of movement and she could not drag her legs across the room. She turned to face Miss Vining who at that time began to wrestle around in her bed. However, the nurse was unable to reach out to her, and had to sit back into the chair from whence she had come. Within seconds she mysteriously fell asleep.

When the nurse awoke she found Miss Vining to have a raging temperature. She was also delirious and was flapping her arms and legs as she rumbled around the bed. At length the nurse managed to calm her and the patient fell asleep once more. The nurse related her experience to the doctor, who told her that under no circumstances were there to be any visitors to Miss Vining. He instructed her to lock the door that evening.

When the nurse settled down to while away the hours until bedtime she again passed her time reading. Once more she looked up and saw the little girl. When she tried to make her way to the girl she held up her hand again, and the nurse found that she had lost all the power in her legs. Almost simultaneously Miss Vining became restless. Her delirium grew to such a state that the nurse tried with all her might to reach the bed, but the spell the child had placed her under meant that she was unable to move. The nurse looked back at the little girl who by this time had moved from her seat. She made her way towards the window and tried to open it. The nurse now found that her feet could move, and she became frightened that the little girl would be able to open the window and perhaps fall out. She lunged forward towards the girl, but as she tried to grab her she knocked off the large hat she had been wearing.

The nurse was distressed to discover that the girl's head was ghostly white. Her eyes were dark and deep, and the skin was corpse-like. Even more sickening was the sight of her neck, which was gashed from one side to the other. The nurse reckoned that she was of Italian origin from her colouring, but she could watch her no more for she fainted at the sight.

When the nurse eventually came round the girl had vanished. She dragged herself to her feet and made her way towards Miss Vining. The patient was dead, her hands and body cold to the touch. The nurse fled the room to relate the tale to the doctor.

Later, when the hotel staff tidied up Miss Vining's belongings they discovered an old faded photograph. It showed a young girl which the nurse was able to confirm was the very same as the girl she had witnessed. Written on the back of the photograph were five mystifying words, 'Natalie. May God forgive us'. There was nothing else to identify the girl, and her story was never discovered.

The Cobbler Hotel at Arrochar in Argyll was originally the family seat of the chiefs of the MacFarlane clan. The house was erected in 1697, though it has been extended a number of times since. In the eighteenth century the Colquhouns of Luss acquired the house, and it is here that one of the chiefs seems to have preferred to live. Colquhoun's wife was at the time having an illicit affair with one of her neighbours. One night Colquhoun arrived at the house, only to find his wife and the neighbour in a compromising position. In a rage he drew his sword and killed the man. The sword wounded his wife, who had run screaming towards him to try and prevent the murder. With blood pouring from her body she felt her way along a corridor to one of the bedrooms. Collapsing on a bed, she expired.

The spirit of the Colquhoun wife was to remain at the house thereafter. Reports of a Green Lady were made over the years, but she seemed only to appear when a member of the family was about to die. There are many other accounts of 'Heralds of Death' amongst the landed gentry.

There are other accounts as to why the house is haunted by a Green Lady. Another version states that a daughter of the MacFarlane chief fell in love with a son of the Colquhoun family. Because of the enmity between the two families all meetings had to be clandestine. However, the MacFarlane chief discovered that his daughter was having a romance of which he disapproved. He warned the girl never to see the MacFarlane lad again, but she was to ignore her father's admonition. When her father discovered that she had ignored him he was so incensed that he had her locked up in one of the house's rooms. She was given no food or water for some days, and after a short time died. Since that time it has been claimed that her manifestation wanders the hotel as a Green Lady.

Another Green Lady haunts Thainstone House Hotel, which stands within its policies to the south of Inverurie in Aberdeenshire. The spirit has been seen a number of times by guests at the hotel, as well as by the house's previous owners, and all describe her as having a green-coloured cloak over her shoulders. She is also dressed as though she is about to go riding, with leather boots and jodhpurs. The ghost is thought to be that of a daughter of the owners who was last seen alive wearing that garb. She left the house and mounted a horse in the stables, which she rode along the drives within the estate. Unfortunately, she fell from her mount, and the injury was such that she died almost instantly. The corpse was brought back to the house and laid out in what is now Room 406. It is this room that seems to have the greatest number of happenings.

Another account as to the origin of the spectre dates from the Jacobite risings. During that time the Jacobites set the house on fire. A daughter of the family preferred to die in the flames rather than face some unknown torture at their hands.

A couple stayed in Room 406, which is furnished as a twin room. During the night the husband awoke to discover a weight on top of him. At first he thought it was his wife being a bit amorous, coming to visit him in the middle of the night, but something made him discard this idea. He tried to get up to switch on the lamp, but found movement difficult due to the weight on him. As he struggled it gradually released, and he was able to rise. Once the lamp was switched on he found that the room was totally silent and empty, apart from his wife sleeping soundly on the other bed.

One of the witnesses who saw the Green Lady watched in awe as she passed across a room and walked through a closed door. On one occasion a night porter that saw her was so frightened that he left the hotel in a hurry. He returned the following day to collect his belongings and vowed he would never go back. When Derrick Phillips was dining at the hotel in 1995 he entered the billiard room and instantly felt an uneasiness that he could not explain by rational means. Richie Tait, from Inverurie, worked as a relief porter at the hotel. On one of the nights he was working he was preparing a table in the Upper Gallery at half past three in the morning. As he finished the task he turned suddenly and walked through the middle of what seemed to be smoke in the shape of a human. Taken aback at this, he blurted out the apology, 'Christ, I'm sorry mate!' thinking that he had just bumped into someone. However, he quickly appreciated that there was no one there, and on turning round to see what it was, nothing could be seen.

Some folk think that the Green Lady is irritated by the presence of women in some of the rooms. A recent resident found that the glass on the dressing-table had been smashed whilst she had been dining and no one had been in her room. The contents of the lady's make-up bag had also been tipped out. In Room 406 pieces of furniture are sometimes moved around when the room is empty. These can be as large as sideboards, tables or chairs. On other occasions the tops of tables or dressing-tables have been swept of all articles on them. However, no one has ever seen this taking place. At various times parts of the hotel turn icy cold for no apparent reason.

John Clark of Torphins works as a porter at the hotel. One night, when only two guests were still awake, he left them to attend to some other chores. As he made his way along the corridor he heard a soft voice calling 'John'. The sound seemed to be coming from a female, and from the direction of the main stairway. However, realizing that the only two guests awake at the hotel were back in the lounge he returned that way to see what they wanted. However, they had not called for him nor heard the voice themselves. On another occasion John was folding the daily newspapers early in the morning. He left the task to answer the telephone and on returning discovered that one of the papers had folded itself and moved to the rack where it should go.

Thainstone also seems to suffer from some poltergeist activity, for there have been reports made of objects moving by themselves. These can take the form of various things, and the occurrences have taken place in various rooms within the house. There is one room in particular, however, which dogs are scared to enter. On numerous occasions the animals have walked happily by their owners' sides, only to halt suddenly as this room is reached. They begin snarling and barking, their hair standing on end, and even when being dragged by a leash, refuse to cross the threshold.

Richie Tait has also witnessed strange occurrences at the Grampian Hotel in Aberdeen. This building was formerly known as the Imperial Hotel, and it is claimed that it occupies the site of an old monastery. The apparition here is thought to have some connection with the ecclesiastical buildings. One of the rooms in part of the building that is now unused is known as the Haunted Room.

According to the locals, a Green Lady reputedly haunts Huntly Castle Hotel, which stands outside the Aberdeenshire town of Huntly. In her earthly life she was a servant at what was a country seat belonging to the Duke of Gordon. She fell pregnant whilst still unmarried, and the local gossip claimed that it was one of the gentry who had got her into this condition. With the stories going the rounds, she became ever more embarrassed and ultimately killed herself.

The Green Lady at Tulloch Castle Hotel, at Dingwall in Ross-shire, is the spirit of a young girl who lived in the Victorian years, when the castle was still the seat of the Davidson family. She had been wandering through the castle and had entered a room where she interrupted her father's secret goings-on with another woman. In her horror at the sight, she ran from the room as fast as she was able. At the principal staircase in the house she stumbled, and fell headlong down a full flight of stairs. The injuries she received resulted in her death.

Tulloch Castle contains fragments of a twelfth century building, but most of the present structure dates from 1891 when the old four-square tower was extended. During the Second World War the castle was used as a hospital, and a number of soldiers being treated there made sightings of the spirit. They were able to identify the girl from a portrait that still hangs within the castle. It is deemed significant that the child is the only figure appearing in the family portrait whose eyes seem to follow you as you walk past it. One of the rooms in the castle is named the 'Green Lady's Lounge' after the resident spectre.

A Grey Lady haunts the Singlie House Hotel in the Borders. The hotel is located in Ettrickdale, south-west of Selkirk. Of this spectre's history nothing seems to be known. Another unknown Grey Lady haunts the Kilmichael Hotel at Brodick on the Island of Arran. This spirit has made a few appearances in certain rooms of the hotel, which was formerly a small country house.

Two spirits haunt the Ravenswood Hotel at Ballater on Royal Deeside. This house dates from around 1820 and was built as a private residence, only being converted into a hotel in the 1970s. One of Ravenswood's manifestations is of a male ghost, who appears most often on the principal staircase of the hotel. Other sightings have taken place in two of the hotel's bedrooms. All who have witnessed this ghost describe him as having the appearance of a sailor. He is an old man, sporting a long white beard, and seems not to wish to cause any harm. The hoteliers have christened him 'Henry', and the room over the main entrance to the hotel has been named 'Henry's Room' in his honour.

Ravenswood's second ghost is thought to be female, but this spirit has never been seen. The only evidence of her existing takes place when baby listening services are offered when children are sleeping in the rooms. Intercoms are set up, so that the parents can listen in elsewhere. On a number of occasions the parents are taken aback when they hear what sounds like a nanny talking to their sleeping child. On investigation, the room is still locked, no one is present, and the child is sleeping soundly.

Another spirit haunts a room within the Pittodrie House Hotel in Aberdeenshire that formerly served as a nursery. The room is no longer in use as such, but the ghost of a nanny still makes odd appearances, as if she is looking for a child to care for. Tradition claims that the nanny was killed falling down the stairs when trying to escape a fire that took place about 1640. The house is centred on an old tower house, but has been extended a number of times since. In recent years strange burning smells, screams and phantom footsteps have been experienced in the vicinity of the old spiral staircase.

Another ghostly nanny or nursery governess is said to haunt the Cally Palace Hotel, which stands in extensive grounds outside Gatehouse of Fleet in Galloway. The house dates from 1763, having been built for James Murray. Tradition claims that a man murdered the governess by throwing her from a fourth floor room in the building. A guest at the hotel around 1975 saw a woman dressed in green being pursued by a man, his arms outstretched and dripping with blood. Sightings of either figure seem not to have happened since.

North of Ballater, at Forbestown in Strathdon, is the Colquhonnie Hotel. The spirit that haunts this hotel seems to have moved from the old Colquhonnie Castle, which dates from the sixteenth century. According to the story told locally, the castle was never completed, and three of the owners who were supervising the masons at work died mysteriously. The ghost, however, is not of one of the lairds, but of his piper. The man was employed by the Forbes laird to play the pipes from the battlement of the tower, but he stumbled and fell over the unfinished parapet, dying as he hit the ground below. This is said to have occurred sometime in the seventeenth century. Since that time the sound of a phantom piper has been heard in the locality. The piper has been witnessed in the Colquhonnie Hotel, which is the nearest substantial building to the ruins of the old castle.

Cameron House Hotel on the shores of Loch Lomond is one of the most luxurious hotels in the country. The house was built in 1830 and extended in 1865 for the Smollett family, one of the most famous members of which was the novelist Tobias Smollett. One of the bedrooms in the house experiences rather strange phenomena, and many guests there have been startled by what they witness. Guests in the room spot an object sitting on a table or other surface — something that they know does not belong to them. Wondering how it might have got there, they are tempted to reach out and lift it, only for it to fade away before their eyes.

Another luxury hotel is the Dryburgh Abbey Hotel, which stands by the side of the River Tweed, near St Boswells in the Borders. The hotel is a rather grand baronial mansion of 1892 which has long served as a hotel. The house occupies the site of a much older building, which was in existence in the sixteenth century when the adjacent abbey was still functional. One of the monks from the abbey became friendly with a daughter from the house and after a time they fell in love. The abbot of Dryburgh found out about this illicit affair and, to try and prevent the scandal from becoming common knowledge in the district, he arranged to have the monk killed. This duly took place and it was passed off as a murder committed by a stranger to the area.

The monk's girlfriend, however, could not accept her lover's death, and after spending a few weeks in mourning committed suicide by throwing herself into the River Tweed. Her lifeless body was found miles downstream from the spot where she had entered the water. Although her corpse was laid to rest, her soul failed to find peace, and her spirit haunted the vicinity of her home thereafter. At the spot where she had thrown herself into the river a suspension bridge was later erected, and the spirit of Dryburgh's Grey Lady has regularly been seen there. Other sightings have been reported in a few outbuildings of the hotel, no doubt within those parts of the hotel that stand on the site of the original house.

In 1993, when the hotel was subject to some major restoration work, the ghost seemed to increase its appearances. Workmen regularly reported tools going missing or equipment being tampered with, even when it was known that no one had been near them. The manager of the hotel was in the building one evening and sensed that someone was following him. He was perturbed at this, for he knew that he should have been in the building alone. The impression that someone else was in the building was so strong that he checked all the windows and doors for signs of being tampered with, but found nothing. Whether it is just to placate guests or not, the hotel claims that she must have been satisfied with the renovations, for she has not been seen since.

The Cathedral House Hotel stands in Cathedral Square in Glasgow, at the top end of the oldest part of the city. Guests and staff at the hotel have seen the ghosts of two children in the building, but nothing seems to be known of who they might have been in life.

Another city hotel also claims to be haunted. The Hilton Hotel is a modern tower block building that is home to at least two ghosts: one male, the other female. The male spirit seems to appear in the bar, where reports of glasses moving by themselves and lights switching themselves on and off have been noted. More frightening, however, is the fact that items in the bar have been known to fly across the room for no apparent reason. The spirit here is said to groan at men, but wolf-whistle at female staff! A barmaid employed at the hotel became so scared of the constant attention she was receiving that she fled from her work.

The Hilton's second ghost takes the form of an attractive female. She wears a shimmering blue dress that is low cut at the front and her long golden hair cascades down over her shoulders. This ghost is friendlier than the spirit in the bar, and hotel staff have claimed that they quite often receive bookings for rooms on the thirteenth floor by folk desperate to witness this spectre. Claims that the Hilton Hotel is haunted have existed almost since it was erected.

In Kinross-shire the Nivingston House Hotel is home to the spectral figure of an old woman. She appears irregularly, but has been seen in various parts of the old section of the hotel, which is centred on an old mansion of 1725 that lies at the foot of the Cleish Hills. Who the spirit was in real life is not known, but she tends to manifest in the same two bedrooms. One of these was formerly a bathroom, and the spirit often passes from one to the other. Although the spectre here is reckoned to be female, the only real tragedy known to have occurred in these rooms took place in the early twentieth century when the owner of Nivingston is thought to have committed suicide by shooting himself. In 1994 the players from Raith Rovers Football Club were staying at Nivingston on the night before an important cup tie. Some of the strapping football players allegedly became so frightened in one of their rooms that they pushed the twin beds together and preferred to sleep all night with the lights on just in case the old woman made an appearance. Fortunately for them she did not!

The Knipoch Hotel is located on the southern shores of Loch Feochan, six miles south of Oban in Argyll. It occupies the site of an older house that was the scene of a murder on 4 February 1592. John Campbell of Cawdor was spending the night at the home of his son-in-law, Dugald Campbell of Glenfeochan. Three shots were fired through the window, one of which killed Cawdor. The conspirators were later caught and taken to Inveraray and placed on trial. The spirit of Cawdor is said to haunt Knipoch Hotel since that time.

The Dreadnought Hotel in the Perthshire resort of Callander is a popular haunt of the tourist who is travelling around the southern highlands. Francis MacNab, chief of the clan, built the hotel in 1802, but it was extended considerably in 1896. The name comes from the motto on the chief's armorial bearings. The oldest part of the hotel has a long reputation for being haunted by a female spirit, and tradition claims that Francis was a fiery character. Different accounts exist as to why the hotel is haunted, from MacNab bricking up his wife in one of the rooms and leaving her to die, to him throwing a hotel maid out of a window after she had become pregnant by him.

Other manifestations have taken place in the Dreadnought. There is an ancient well in the cellars of the hotel, from when there was no public water supply, and it is said that a child was drowned here — perhaps another love-child of MacNab's. In one of the bedrooms the sound of a sobbing infant has often been heard, and it is thought that it comes from the spirit of the infant in the well. MacNab himself is said to wander the corridors of the old building, and a portrait of him that hangs in the hotel is said to move at the same time as his ghost is ranging through the corridors.

4

Poltergeist Activity

The term poltergeist is from the German and translates into English as 'noisy ghost'. Very often the spirits that haunt buildings may not be seen, and those who experience them are only aware of sounds. These vary from banging, scraping, footsteps and smashing glass, to music, knocks and thuds. Poltergeist activity can also be witnessed on occasions, and a number of reports have been made of things moving mysteriously across rooms. This activity can be quite violent, with objects being smashed into walls, or items as large as pieces of furniture being knocked over.

Poltergeist activity is sometimes associated with a person rather than a specific place. There are many folk who claim that objects have moved in their presence, not necessarily in the same place, and that others present at the time have witnessed this.

An old account of poltergeist activity was made in 1655. Apparently a tinker, or travelling packman, had arrived at the house of Gilbert Campbell, which stood in the

Wigtownshire village of Glenluce. Campbell refused to buy any of his wares, and in the discussion was said to have insulted the packman, Alexander Agnew. Agnew then placed a curse on Campbell's home before leaving.

Soon after this had taken place, Campbell noticed things in his house were not the same. It started when objects were thrown at the outside wall of the building, and against the shutters of the windows. Then problems were experienced inside the house. Clothing would be found shredded to bits and the bedclothes would suddenly throw themselves from the beds. The poltergeist activity at Glenluce continued for some time, until Alexander Agnew was apprehended and hanged. The curse was broken, and Gilbert Campbell was then able to lead an undisturbed life.

Another very old reference to poltergeists dates from the year after the haunting at Glenluce. In 1656 Gilbert Imlach lived in the parish of Cullen, on the Banffshire coast. Some form of spectre seemed to live in his cottage and was responsible for making lumps of peat fly across the room or else move in the air outside. On other occasions the ghost talked to him. This seemed to bother him for some time, and eventually he was brought before the kirk session. They suspected his wife, Margaret Philp, and made out that she was a witch of sorts. Whether she was punished or not is not known, but there are no more references to the strange activity at their cottage in the session minutes.

One of the strangest cases that linked poltergeist activity with a person occurred at Park Crescent in Sauchie in Clackmannanshire in 1960. A girl of eleven years of age seemed to attract paranormal activity. Strange sounds could be heard at times when she was present, and it was also noted that large objects would sometimes move by themselves. Virginia Campbell had moved with her family from County Donegal in Ireland in recent months to settle in the small village outside Alloa. It was thought that the move, and the loss of her dog, which was left behind in Ireland, could have been partially responsible for the strange happenings.

Mrs Annie Campbell sent for her family practitioner to ask for advice. Dr William Nisbet of Tillicoultry examined the girl, but he could find no signs of anything physically wrong with her. He consulted with a colleague, Dr William Logan, and a local minister, Revd Thomas Lund, and together they decided to try out a few experiments.

The loss of the dog was thought to be a

major factor in the sudden commencement of the poltergeist activity. It has often been claimed that major traumatic events (such as death or murder) can create a strange form of energy that results in spirits. The doctor wondered whether this might have been the case with the loss of Virginia's dog. To try and get rid of the upset he decided to let Virginia borrow his own dog for a while. The girl was delighted, but it had no effect on the activity.

The doctor then decided to try a few drugs. Each time that objects moved in her vicinity the girl was in a hysterical state. He thought that the girl's mind might be creating the illusion of the moving objects, and to try and prevent this he prescribed sedatives. Even when the girl remained calm the sounds and movements still occurred.

Another experiment involved removing the girl from her environment. She was sent to live with a relative in the neighbouring village of Dollar for two nights. Despite being more than three miles away from her home the poltergeist activity continued. Dr Logan and his wife visited the girl at Dollar and they too witnessed the sounds. They also reported that the girl began to speak in a manner too old for her age. It was stated that it seemed as though the girl's body had been taken over by an adult spirit that spoke in a more mature language.

The strange activity followed Virginia to Sauchie Primary School. Her teacher, Miss Margaret Stewart, witnessed a bowl full of hyacinths moving across her desk. Virginia was standing near to her at the time, and the movement was put down to her. On other occasions Virginia's desk or its lid would move up by itself and she had to forcibly hold it down.

On 1 December 1960, the Revd Thomas Lund and two friends paid the Campbell household a visit. They held a service by her bedside in which they prayed for the girl, asking the evil spirits to come out of her. Although the poltergeist activity did not stop instantly at that time, it subsided considerably. It had been at its peak for about one week beforehand. Thereafter, over a period of a year, until March 1962, the strange occurrences faded away, until they eventually stopped.

The strange occurrences at Sauchie have been captured on film. The Revd Lund was able to use a cine camera to capture the sight of boxes opening by themselves, covers on beds rippling without anyone near them and pillows moving unaided. He also taped the strange sounds experienced, which included bouncing and sawing noises.

Another modern poltergeist case took place in the 1980s at Bainsford, near Falkirk. A woman in her thirties lived in a flat there alone. The activity did not start as soon as she moved in to the flat, but built up over the years. Some of the most unusual sights were a red glow that moved around the sitting room and a mist that hovered around the bedroom. One day mystical writing appeared on the wall — the letters D and E, numbers 32 and 37, plus three crosses. In all, the strange happenings frightened the tenant so much that she left the flat and moved back in with her mother.

Psychic mediums came to the house and one of them spotted the spirit of a soaking child lying on the carpet. This seemed to confirm the rumour that an infant had been drowned, perhaps deliberately, in the bath. After the resident moved out of the flat the haunting seems to have ceased.

Braco Castle in Perthshire is an old building of the sixteenth century to which additions and alterations have been made over the centuries. The oldest part of the castle is said to be the home of a poltergeist that causes doors to open themselves.

Craignethan Castle in Lanarkshire has been mentioned in *Scottish Ghosts* as the home of a White Lady and some weird noises. The custodian lives on site in a building that forms part of the castle, dating from 1661. Also in this building is the castle tearoom, and here a number of guests have received frights. On a few occasions pans have been known to fly off the cooker, and on one occasion Anna Withowski was burned when this happened. Pictures on the wall have been known to move from one place to another. Inexplicable sounds have also been heard as visitors tried to enjoy a cup of tea. The custodian's dog refuses to enter the tearoom, yet quite happily wanders at will round the rest of the castle.

The custodian at Craignethan, Robert Sandilands, tells visitors that he often gets a deathly chill when he enters the tearoom. He has heard voices that appear to speak in a strange dialect, yet on checking the building he finds that there is no one present. A number of visitors who have entered the tearoom have also experienced the cold chill and vowed never to return.

Another case of poltergeist activity took place near the Aberdeenshire village of Longside in 1825. James Wylie was the tenant of Boodie Brae croft, which stands in the countryside of the Ugie valley. His cottage was subject to numerous paranormal goings-on. This included tables and chairs moving about the room of their own accord and banging on the floor, even when no one was near them. James Wylie put up with the poltergeist activity for some time. On one occasion a woman paid a visit to the cottage, and a pail full of water lifted itself up from the floor and tipped its contents over her. The strange occurrences continued for six months until James Wylie died.

Busta House in the Shetland Islands dates from 1588, but additions were made to it in 1714 and again in 1984, by which time it had been converted to a country house hotel. Located twenty-three miles or so to the north of Lerwick, Busta House was the property of the Gifford family. In the eighteenth century the owner was Thomas Gifford, who was married to Elizabeth Mitchell. They had fourteen children, of which four were sons. The eldest, and heir to the estates, John, caused his mother considerable grief, for he fell in love with a distant cousin, an orphan child named Barbara Pitcairn. Although a member of the family, she was employed in the house as a maidservant and as a companion to Thomas's wife. She disliked the thought of John forming a relationship with Barbara, and was heard to relate that she would rather see her son dead at her feet than have him marry the maidservant.

On 14 May 1748 John Gifford, his three brothers, their tutor and the boatman sailed across the Busta Voe to Wethersta where a number of relatives lived. Although it was a calm night and the sea was peaceful, the sailors failed to return home. At daybreak a search party was sent out to look for them, riding along the shores of the voe (a Shetland term for a sea-loch) to see if their bodies had been washed ashore. Someone found the boat, which was still sailing upright. Within it they discovered John's walking stick and hat, but no sign of anything else. After a short time the bodies of John Gifford and the tutor were washed ashore. Nothing was ever found of the other four. Elizabeth was distraught with grief. Her son and heir had drowned, along with his brothers, and there were only girls to inherit the lands.

However, the eldest son, John, had secretly married Barbara Pitcairn, who was now pregnant by him. She told the laird and his wife this, and they took her in. In time a son, Gideon, was born. Thomas Gifford and his wife accepted this child as rightful heir, but they could not bring themselves to be civil to Barbara. She was spurned in the house, and forced to move to Lerwick where she lived with relatives for a time. Gideon remained at Busta where the Giffords brought him up. He was to meet his mother only once after she moved away, when he was seven years old. Barbara died of a broken heart at Lerwick at the early age of thirty-five.

Some folk claim that Barbara Pitcairn and John Gifford were not indeed married. They say that when she went to Busta to tell the grieving parents that she was pregnant by their son, they had either assumed that they had been secretly married, or else used this tale to legitimize the bastard child. The doubt over whether Gideon was in fact legitimate resulted in a major lawsuit brought against him by a cousin, who would have inherited the estates if he had been a natural child. This lawsuit took ninety-three years to resolve, but by that time the costs had brought the family to ruin and the house fell into disrepair.

After Barbara's death her spirit managed to make its way back to Busta where it appeared on a regular basis, haunting the elder Giffords. Many claimed that the ghost was back to see her son, watching to make sure that he was brought up properly. It is said that her manifestation continues to wander the building searching for him. Many guests at the house have reported seeing her. In recent years she has appeared in the bar of the hotel, where a young child saw her and thought that she was so real that she offered her something to eat. Other guests in the room did not see anything.

There may be a second ghost at Busta. In the Linga Room various guests have claimed that they awoke during the night to see an older woman at the foot of the bed. She is dressed in brown with a lace cap covering most of her grey hair. It has been speculated that this might be the ghost of Elizabeth Gifford, the woman who so badly treated Barbara. Her spirit does not seem to cause any harm, however.

Busta is also home to other paranormal activity. Some poltergeist activity has been reported, mainly in an apartment named the Foula Room. When the room is known to be empty, the sound of footsteps within it can still be made out. Other activity includes electrical items switching themselves on or off. Some say that reports of this nature are more common in the month of May, when the great tragedy befell the family.

Another Shetland poltergeist was active in the late eighteenth century. Ollaberry school was located near the head of the Bay of Ollaberry, which is about ten miles further north from Busta, near the north end of the mainland. At the time of the activity the schoolmaster was James Manson, who lived in the adjoining schoolhouse. During his period at the school he and his family suffered a long spell of poltergeist activity. This was similar to other cases — pots and pans were thrown across the floor, clothing was inexplicably ripped to shreds, bumps and thuds were often heard and crockery smashed. The Manson family tholed this for some time but the activity seemed to get worse. On some occasions the Manson children were subject to being thrown across the room, and they suffered bruising or cuts to their skin.

Various folk tried to help. A strong man from the islands tried to cast out the poltergeist. He held one of the Manson daughters on his knee with great strength, but still the poltergeist managed to wrest the young girl from him. The local minister was called and he tried to calm the activity, but to no avail. At length he suggested inviting a local old woman to the house who was suspected of witchcraft. He told the family to treat her to a meal, but halfway through one of them must lift a burning peat and throw it at her.

The meal went ahead as planned, and Mrs Manson was given the job of throwing the peat at the old woman. It landed in her lap, setting fire to her apron. The old lady jumped up and managed to drop the peat to the floor, all the while slapping at her clothes to put out the flames. The old lady never went back to the house and it is recorded that the Mansons were never bothered by poltergeists again.

Luffness House stands on the edge of the East Lothian village of Aberlady. The building as it is today is of considerable antiquity, but it occupies the site (and no doubt part of the original construction) of the ancient Luffness Castle, which was erected in the thirteenth century. The house has a small room in one of the towers, access to which can only be had through one doorway. On one occasion the owners of the house were amazed to discover that the large and heavy door to this room was locked. No one could remember locking the door, and the key was nowhere to be found. After some time trying to work out who had locked the door, and where they had put the key, someone decided to look through the keyhole. To their amazement, lying on a table within the room was the only key to the door. How it could have got there was a complete mystery, for apart from through the locked door there was no way into the room. Eventually, a poltergeist or some other form of paranormal activity was blamed.

There are two shops in south-west

Scotland that are haunted by some form of poltergeist activity. The first of these occupies a 200-year-old building in the Galloway town of Dalbeattie, which lies thirteen miles south-west of Dumfries. In 1995 Linda Williamson discovered on a number of occasions that the contents of her shop had been tampered with by some unknown spirit. Previously Ms Williamson had experienced odd occurrences that she was unable to explain away. These were generally minor things, such as lights being switched on which she was sure were off, and doors found open which had been left closed. However in November 1995 things took a turn for the worse.

One morning when she arrived to open the shop, she discovered that there were a number of items of clothing lying on the floor of the premises. Linda Williamson thought that the shop had been broken into but there was no apparent evidence of this. On the next day she arrived to discover that hanks of wool had been moved to different places within the shop, and items of baby clothing had been dropped on the floor. On the third day, the wedding gowns that were stocked were discovered to be in a different place to where they had been left the previous night.

Although Ms Williamson could find no sign

of a break-in, she called the local constabulary. They went over the business premises in considerable detail but they, too, could find no sign of any forced entry. They were completely baffled and could not come up with a reasonable explanation. Even the money which had been in the till overnight on the first occasion was still there, and nothing was ever discovered to be missing.

Linda Williamson called in the services of a local priest to exorcize the shop in an attempt to put an end to the problem. Canon Kevin Conway performed this ceremony within the premises and this seems to have brought the strange occurrences to an end.

In the Ayrshire town of Dalry is the ironmonger's owned by John Woodside. Some form of spirit seems to haunt this shop and has been known to move things around on more than one occasion. On a number of mornings, John or his wife Sheena have opened the shop to find that various items have been lifted from the shelves and left on the floor. Wire baskets have been found lying in the aisles and on other occasions shoes were discovered where they should not have been. No sign of a forced entry was apparent, and the moving objects did not set off the burglar alarm.

Edinburgh has a seemingly greater share of

Scotland's spectres than anywhere else. Poltergeist activity is also rife in the city, and many accounts of things moving by themselves have been reported over the centuries.

In 1958, strange occurrences commenced in a Victorian tenement in Rothesay Place. The Van Horne family, who lived at number five, had purchased some second-hand furniture that had previously belonged to a sailor who had recently passed away. Soon after the furniture was delivered, strange things began to happen. Sounds, which could not be explained by normal means, were heard. These were usually tapping sounds. Then ornaments that had been placed on the sailor's furniture were discovered located in different places.

In July 1958 the Van Hornes began smelling tobacco smoke in their home. On further inquiry it was discovered that the sailor had been renowned for smoking a pipe. Things then got suddenly worse. A bright ball of light was spotted in the house, and it seemed to move from room to room. In September that year a tiny male figure made an appearance. This figure was only about one foot in height and he was dressed in a brown jacket with red trousers. From his appearance the Van Hornes nicknamed him 'Gnomey'. This figure made a number of appearances, and was witnessed by various members of the family. By the beginning of the 1960s the haunting at Rothesay Place came to an end, almost as suddenly as it had started.

In Hazeldean Terrace, poltergeist activity also took place at number five. The first indication of a strange presence was when a wooden chopping-board seemed to jump from where it lay and crashed to the floor. The board was positioned in such a manner that it had not simply fallen over, but required some form of force to lift it. This took place in 1957. Within a short time the board had mysteriously moved once more, and on a number of occasions it had bounced across the room and hit the kitchen table, leaving dents on the surface. Other items then joined in — glasses and cups were found to have moved, and to have been broken in two pieces. The break was unusual in that it was a neat split, and not a shatter.

The family who lived at 5 Hazeldean Terrace put up with the happenings in their house for some time. Even when they lay in bed at night they could hear strange noises coming from the kitchen. These varied from thuds and bangs, to items of glassware or ceramics being broken. Again, like in Rothesay Place, the activity came to an abrupt end in the early 1960s.

5

Ancient Apparitions

Ghosts are usually associated with ancient buildings, such as castles, and Scotland has more than its fair share of these. Virtually every one seems to have its own ghost story, and the following examples can only be a selection from the hundreds that exist. The reader can find many more haunted castles in the author's previous book, *Scottish Ghosts*. Here, our tour round the castles will commence in south-west Scotland, cross to the Borders, go up the east coast towards Caithness, before returning down the west side of the country.

At Ardrossan, on the Ayrshire coast, the ruins of Ardrossan castle stand on a low hilltop. The castle has long been in ruins, but at one time was a seat of the Barclay family and one of the most important fortresses in the area. In the late thirteenth century the castle fell into English hands. William Wallace, the great Scots freedom fighter, attacked the foe whilst they occupied the castle. He was so successful that he left the entire garrison of soldiers for dead. The corpses were dragged from the building and taken down into the basement, where they were piled up on each other. So numerous were the bodies that the vault was filled to overflowing. Since that time this part of the castle has been known as Wallace's Larder.

It is not ghosts of Englishmen that are said to haunt Ardrossan; rather it is the manifestation of Wallace himself. Locals claim that his spirit manifests on stormy nights, wandering among the ruins.

On the edge of the Ayrshire town of Kilmarnock stands Dean Castle, an ancient square keep to which 'palace' blocks and courtyard walls were later added. It was the seat of the Boyds of Kilmarnock, who seem to have been involved in every major part of Scottish history, from Wallace and Bruce to Mary Queen of Scots, Cromwell, the Covenanters and the Jacobite risings. The castle stood in ruins for a number of years but was restored at the end of the twentieth century by Lord Howard de Walden and later gifted by him to the town. Today it forms the centrepiece of a country park.

In the eighteenth century William Boyd, 4th Earl of Kilmarnock, owned the castle. He was a keen Jacobite and served as Privy

Councillor to Prince Charles Edward Stewart. Whilst the Earl was still alive the servants in the castle experienced a number of strange sightings. On more than one occasion they saw a ghostly head, which looked exactly like Lord Kilmarnock's, rolling about on the floor. At the neck it was dripping with blood and the eyes were rolled up into their sockets. After a few moments the apparition disappeared, leaving the servants in a terrified state.

When Lord Kilmarnock joined the Jacobites in their uprising he remarked to the Earl of Galloway that this had occurred. Lord Galloway responded by saying that it was probably a sign that Boyd would lose his head at some time in the future. After the Battle of Culloden in 1746 the Earl had to flee the field to try and protect his life. He was captured however, and following sentencing, he was beheaded, as predicted by the scenes at his home. As he stood before the chopping block, Lord Kilmarnock told the gathered crowd of the premonition. He stated that he was quite willing to face death, but as his final request he asked that four men be allowed to hold a sheet in order to catch his head once it was separated from his body. This was because he could not stand the thought of it rolling about on the floor.

Not all of the inexplicable happenings in the Dean Castle are connected with the grisly execution of the last earl. In the Palace block, which dates from around 1460, the faint sound of music playing has sometimes been heard. When those who are unaware of this strange phenomenon hear it, they often try to find out where it comes from, but despite searching the building, no source for it can be found.

In the suburbs of the city of Glasgow stand the ruins of Crookston Castle. The massive pile of the ancient tower commands a man-made motte hill, and the whole site is protected by Historic Scotland. In the late 1940s, a young boy called Duncan Lindsay lived in one of the adjacent houses, for the lands around the castle are now occupied by one of Glasgow's large housing estates. He was often sent to his bed before he felt that he should go, so he spent his time looking out of the upstairs window. On a number of occasions he witnessed soldiers marching up and down the embankments below the castle.

Dunskey Castle stands on a cliff top to the south of Portpatrick in Wigtownshire. The castle dates from the sixteenth century, but has long been in ruins. Probably built by the Adair family, it was later owned by the Hunter Blairs. The remains were sold in recent years and the new owner has plans to restore the building to a habitable condition. It is claimed that some of the early owners of the castle captured the abbot of Soulseat Abbey and held him prisoner in the castle. He was tortured for some time, in an attempt to persuade him to sign over the abbey lands. Eventually he did so, and since that time there have been tales of the castle being haunted by the screaming abbot. This tale is quite suspect, for a similar story is told of Dunure Castle in Ayrshire, on which there is more documentary evidence.

Dunskey is also said to have had a 'brownie' ghost that appeared during the night and carried out chores on behalf of the owners. Other accounts claim that a child's nurse also haunted the building. She is said to have been holding the child rather too near the window, when the infant began to struggle and fell to its death on the rocks below. Again this tale has been recounted at other castles, in particular at Duntulm Castle on Skye.

Lochhouse Tower is a solitary square keep standing one mile to the south of Moffat in Dumfriesshire. The tower was restored in 1973 and is occupied as a family house. Lochhouse was erected sometime in the sixteenth century by the Johnstones of that ilk. Around the end of the sixteenth century Lilias Johnstone lived in the castle. She was a beautiful woman, and she fell in love with a near neighbour, Walter French of Frenchland Tower. Walter proposed to Lilias, but her brother, who had succeeded as the laird of Lochhouse, did not think much of Walter. The pair of them quarrelled over the matter, this building up into a fight in which Johnstone was killed.

Walter French was so overcome with remorse that he decided to head overseas where he served in the army. He felt that Lilias would never fully love him for having killed her brother. Other accounts claim that Walter French subsequently returned to Annandale and married a daughter of the laird of Breckonside.

Lilias Johnstone still loved Walter, but was unable to marry him. She was still a beautiful woman, and many men tried to woo her, but to no avail. She remained in Lochhouse Tower, pining for her lover, until she eventually died. From that time her spirit has haunted the tower. An old poem tells her tale:

Fair Lilias sits in Lochhouse Tower,
Her cheek is wet and pale,
And a' her happiness is fled,
The Flower of Annandale.

Why does she languish in her bower,
And saut tears fill her e'e?
Alack she greets and pines for ane,
She never mair may see.

Cranshaws Tower stands on the side of one of the Lammermuir Hills, in the remote vale of Whiteadder Water, at the northern end of Berwickshire. The castle is a rather simple tower house of the fifteenth century, standing 65 ft in height and measuring 40 by 24 ft in plan. A more modern mansion superseded it. Tradition in the area claims that the castle was home to one of the strange paranormal creatures known in Scotland as a 'brownie'. These rarely-seen spirits are supposed to come out at night and carry out work on behalf of the owner. Any comments made about this or any attempt to see them at their work usually results in them withdrawing their services, never to be seen again.

The brownie at Cranshaws appeared at harvest time, when the cornfields were cut and the sheaves left in stacks, awaiting gathering. During the night the corn would mysteriously be threshed and winnowed, ready to be stored for the winter. This seems to have taken place over many years at Cranshaws, and the owners were quite happy to let it happen. One year, unfortunately for the owners, a servant in the tower commented that the corn had not been stacked as neatly as it usually was. The brownie heard this comment, and was incensed at the words. Deciding that he would never come back again, he vented his anger by throwing the already-gathered sheaves into the Whiteadder Water at a spot two miles from the tower, known as the Raven Craig. His services were never to be offered again.

Thirlestane Castle is a rather grand baronial pile of a building, more like a French château than a traditional Scots tower house. The main part of the castle dates from the sixteenth century, but it has been extended over the years. At one time a seat of the Earls and Duke of Lauderdale, a trust and Gerald Maitland-Carew now own the house jointly.

John Maitland, 2nd Earl and only Duke of Lauderdale, owned Thirlestane in the seventeenth century. He was an important politician at the time, becoming Secretary of State in 1661. However, in 1680 he was replaced following the Covenanter rising that began with their victory at the Battle of Drumclog. Lauderdale died in 1682, since which time his ghost is said to haunt both here and St Mary's Church in Haddington. His corpse was laid to rest in the Lauderdale vault there.

Witnesses who have seen the spectre of the Duke of Lauderdale describe him as being rather an important looking figure with long curly hair. A full-length portrait of him that hangs in the castle dining room has proved useful in identifying him as the ghost. He has manifested close to the church of St Mary's, and at Thirlestane he has appeared a number of times in various parts of the castle. The most common location for him to appear is in a room located above what is known as Bonnie Prince Charlie's Room. This room is located on the third floor (where the corridor is known as the 'High Street') but it remains unrestored.

Historic Scotland cares for the impressive ruins of Crichton Castle, which lie in a quiet glen half a mile south of Crichton Church in Midlothian. The castle has a rather fine Italianate façade in its inner courtyard, and what may be the oldest scale and platt stairway in Scotland. On the opposite side of the courtyard is the original vaulted entrance to the castle, long since closed off and converted into a storeroom. Beyond this, south of the castle by a few hundred yards, is another ruin, which was originally a stable connected with the castle. On a few occasions it has been claimed that a figure on horseback has been seen riding from here towards the castle. Witnesses who have seen this only realize fully that it is a manifestation when the mounted figure rides the horse through the wall that blocks off the original gateway.

It is thought that the rider was Sir William Crichton, who was Chancellor of Scotland in the first half of the fifteenth century. He was responsible for organizing the so-called 'Black Dinner' in Edinburgh Castle in 1440. To this the Earl of Douglas and his brother, serious contenders for the crown, were invited. During the meal a prearranged group of mercenaries burst in and murdered the Douglases.

Not too far from Crichton, four miles as the crow flies, is Dalhousie Castle, standing above the River South Esk, near Lasswade. The castle appears to be a mock-Gothic structure, but this hides an ancient building within, parts of which are claimed to date from the thirteenth century. Dalhousie was for centuries home to the Ramsay family, later Earls of Dalhousie, but today is a rather fine country house hotel. One of the early Ramsays was Sir Alexander, who fought in the battles for independence in the fourteenth century. He was captured by Sir William Douglas in 1342 and imprisoned in Hermitage Castle in Roxburghshire, where he was starved to death. His final days were prolonged by the fact that a few grains of corn fell into the dungeon from the granary above, keeping him alive for seventeen days. His spirit is said to haunt Hermitage Castle, wandering among the ruins.

Dalhousie has its own ghost as well. A Grey Lady has been seen in the castle dungeon, as well as on one of the old staircases. Witnesses have also heard the sound of her clothes rustling as she spirited past, as well as other inexplicable noises. The Grey Lady is thought to be the manifestation of a Lady Catherine. Who exactly she was is not known, but it is thought that she was the mistress of one of the lairds. His wife discovered that he was having an affair, and she was able to lure Lady Catherine into the castle on some pretext or other. When she was in one of the turrets the laird's wife locked her up, where she remained until she died of starvation.

In Edinburgh is Craigcrook Castle, located on the slopes of Corstorphine Hill. The castle incorporates an old tower house to which various baronial additions have been made over the years. It is now used as offices. In the nineteenth century Lord Francis Jeffrey lived here, and his spirit is claimed to haunt the building. Jeffrey was Lord Advocate and a notable writer. He died in 1850 aged seventy-six.

The strange occurrences at Craigcrook are numerous. The library has a reputation for suddenly turning rather cold. Noises have been heard throughout the building, and when the source of them is investigated nothing to explain them can be found. These include the sound of footsteps in rooms known to be empty and the ringing of the doorbell when no one is near it. On a number of occasions items have been known to move from one place to another when nobody is there.

To the north of Falkirk is Airth Castle, a rather grand Gothic pile perched on a small hill in the middle of a wide carse. The oldest part of the present building is probably the fourteenth century Wallace's Tower, to which additions have been made over the years. In the seventeenth century a house-keeper was given the job of looking after two children. She was rather lax in this task, and would often leave them to play alone for hours on end. During one of her periods away the children began playing with the fire, causing it to collapse and burn them so severely that they died of their wounds. The housekeeper was so overcome with remorse that she died soon after. Her spirit still haunts the room in the old part of the castle where the children died. Some claim that she is still looking for the children, as if she were unaware that they had been killed.

The ancient kingdom of Fife is home to a number of haunted castles. To the south-west of Kirkcaldy stands Balwearie Castle, an ancient ruin that dates in part from the fifteenth century. The castle site is associated with the so-called wizard, Michael Scott, who lived in the thirteenth century. He had a supernatural ability that earned him his epithet. The ghost at Balwearie has no connections with the wizard, however, other than the fact that they share the same surname. Thomas Scott owned Balwearie in the sixteenth century. He was a justice clerk at the court of James V. When Scott died in 1539, his spirit and the manifestation of little devils appeared before the king, who was in his chamber at Linlithgow Palace at the time. Scott's spirit warned the king that he would face an eternity in hell himself. The ghost of Scott has been claimed to appear at Balwearie on occasion, but those who have seen him do not claim to have witnessed the devils.

Whereas Balwearie is in ruins, Fernie Castle is complete, and is now a luxury hotel. Guests have to be willing to risk seeing the Green Lady, who has a habit of appearing in various bedrooms. Perhaps unconnected with her, but still as frightening to many, is the strange occurrence of lights that switch themselves on and off without warning, or other electrical equipment which does the same.

Fernie's Green Lady is one of many ghosts that have their origin in a lovelorn daughter falling to her death from a tower. The girl fell in love with a son of the castle, but her father disapproved of her choice. She ran away with him and came to his home at Fernie. Her father set off in pursuit and burst into the castle. His followers carried out a search of the building, and as they burst into the room where the lovers were hiding, she tried to escape by jumping from a third floor window in the western tower. Killing herself in the process, her spirit has haunted the castle ever since.

A Green Lady haunts the ruins of Newark Castle, near St Monans in Fife. The locals often speak of the legend, and it is said that the sound of her silken gown may still be heard rustling along the long-since destroyed corridors. The original of the Green Lady is thought to be Jean Leslie, daughter of General Sir David Leslie (d. 1682). 'Green Jean', as she is known, is buried in the graveyard that surrounds the Auld Kirk of St Monans. Why she has chosen to return to her home and wander throughout the ruins no one can tell. Some folk say that the smugglers who used to frequent this part of the Fife coast invented the tale of Newark's Green Lady. There are caves beneath the headland on which the castle stands, and these were often used for landing brandy, rum, and other fine goods.

Between Dunfermline and Rosyth stands the ancient house or castle of Pitreavie, at one time a seat of the Wardlaw family. The house was built in the early part of the seventeenth century but it has been rebuilt since, and buildings associated with the Northern Maritime Air Region Security surround it today. The older part of the house was home to some type of ghost. It seemed to appear most frequently in a small chamber located on the north side of the building. According to David Beveridge, writing in *Between the Ochils and the Forth* in 1888, 'I never could learn what appearance the spirit was supposed to assume; but so fixed and persistent was the belief in it, that not many years ago, when the house was empty, and a number of harvest labourers were bivouacked there, nothing could induce them to do otherwise than congregate together in one large room.' Beveridge also records that, 'A similar visitant was believed formerly to haunt Otterston, but in this case it took the form of a lady with a child in her arms — the victim of misplaced affection.' The remains of Otterston Castle are located immediately north of Dalgety Bay, next to the loch of the same name, and only three miles as the crow flies from Pitreavie.

Dozens of large estates in Perthshire still have ancient castles as the seat. Others are now in ruins, and a number of smaller towers have been restored to create sizeable and distinctive family homes.

Megginch Castle stands on a low knoll in the Carse of Gowrie, the flat stretch of Perthshire that lies north of the Firth of Tay. The castle dates from the fifteenth century and has been a seat of the Drummond family since 1646. Surrounding it are ancient gardens, including yew trees that are said to be at least one thousand years old and a sixteenth century physic garden. The castle itself is a fine structure, though the original tower house was extended considerably in the early nineteenth century. In the oldest part of the building is a room that has a weird atmosphere. Occupants have heard the whispering of what sounds like two old women gossiping to each other. It is not known who they might be, but they have been heard on and off over a long period of time. No one has ever seen anything. The room was at one time a children's nursery, so perhaps the voices heard belong to former nannies who worked there.

Megginch had a long tradition of being haunted, but Admiral Sir Adam Drummond altered the building in the early nineteenth century, sweeping away the ancient rooms and secret passages that the building formerly had. According to Lawrence Melville, writing in *The Fair Land of Gowrie*, this seems to have 'disposed of the legendary 'ghost', for there are now no stories to support the supposition that the castle is the locus of a visitation.' Perhaps the whispering ladies are wondering what happened to the building they once knew.

One of the old towers that have been rebuilt in recent years is Edinample Castle. It stands on the southern shores of Loch Earn, a mile or so from Lochearnhead. The castle is one of seven that Sir Duncan Campbell of Glenorchy (c. 1553–1631) built in the late sixteenth century to guard his ever-increasing estates. His castle building exploits earned him the name 'Black Duncan of the Castles'. Edinample seems to have caused him some problems with the mason, however. The mason was left with instructions on what the laird wanted, but somehow seemed to forget that he demanded a parapet walk. When

Campbell arrived on site and discovered the error he was fired up into a rage. He refused to pay the mason who, rather foolishly, tried to show Campbell that it was possible to walk round the roof. As he scrambled about on the slates Campbell's rage increased, thinking that he was now being made a fool of. Accordingly he pulled his gun and shot the mason, causing him to plummet to the ground below. The spirit of the mason is said to haunt the castle, wandering around on the roof of the Z-plan castle.

The highland town of Aberfeldy has a few castles in its immediate neighbourhood. Grandtully Castle is an ancient structure, distinguished by its tall round tower. Within one of the castle's corner turrets is a mark on the floor that is claimed to be blood shed in a murder. The Battle of Killiecrankie took place on 27 July 1689 between the Jacobites under Viscount Dundee and the supporters of William and Mary under General Hugh Mackay of Scourie. After the initial defeat of the Jacobites, the skirmish spread in a number of directions, the most famous incident being the soldier pursued to a narrow gully where the River Garry makes it way through the rocks. He was able to jump the chasm and thus save his life. Another soldier was pursued as far as Grandtully, where he sought refuge in the tower. The pursuer followed and killed him. The blood that poured from the dead man's corpse left a stain on the floor that has been impossible to remove.

Six miles west of Aberfeldy the road north passes through the narrow Glen of Keltney, or Gleann Mór. On the opposite side of the Keltney Burn, a rather strange tower house can be seen from the road, and was restored in an unusual manner in the 1960s by David Fry. This is Garth Castle, which had a reputation for being home to some rather unruly clansmen. Sir Alexander Stewart, known as the Wolf of Badenoch, built it in the fourteenth century. In the early sixteenth century, Niall (or Nigel) Stewart owned the castle. He was a notorious land-grabber. Stewart captured his neighbour, Sir Robert Menzies, in 1502 and tried to persuade him to sign over some of his lands. Menzies refused, so Stewart had him taken to the dungeon of Garth and locked up.

The ghost of Garth was associated with Stewart in another way. He had fallen out of love with his wife, Mariota, and planned to get rid of her. On 16 August 1545, as she was walking in the deep gully beneath the castle, she was hit on the head by a large stone that could have come from nowhere other than the castle parapet. Although it was widely suspected, no proof could ever link Mariota's death with her husband. Her spirit has remained at Garth, however, where it has been seen wandering amid the trees. Stewart himself was later arrested and imprisoned in his own tower, where he died in 1554.

East of Perthshire is the county of Angus. Almost on the border is Airlie Castle, a seat of the Earl of Airlie. The castle has been in Ogilvie hands since it was built in the fifteenth century. The family seems to have a long tradition of having more than one death herald. One of these takes the form of a drummer boy whose beating can be heard whenever an Earl of Airlie is about to die. This herald is usually heard at Cortachy Castle, one of the family seats. Airlie Castle is home to a different herald of death that takes the form of a ram. Known as the 'Doom of Airlie', the ram is said to make a complete circle of the castle whenever a death is due in the family. The castle stands on a commanding position on a promontory between two rivers, and the ram usually makes its way round the gullies. There have been cases when the ram did not predict a death in the family; instead it intimated that the Ogilvies would suffer some other form of bad fortune.

Another Ogilvie seat in Angus is Inverquharity Castle, at one time owned by Sir John Ogilvie. He was rather keen on a local lass, daughter of the miller. She was what has been described as a beauty, but she seems to have had no real notion for him. Ogilvie tried to persuade her father that he would make a rather fine husband for her, but the miller was unwilling to promote the suitor's case. Ogilvie actually asked the daughter to marry him, but when she refused he made his way to the mill and hanged the miller. He then turned his attentions to the mother, whom he raped, and later carried out the same despicable act on the daughter.

A local priest was informed of Ogilvie's crimes, and he prayed that God would seek vengeance. Accordingly, within a short time Ogilvie died for no apparent reason. His spirit thereafter haunted the castle, and for many months the haunting was so bad that the residents of the castle abandoned it.

Finavon Castle in Angus is said to be haunted by the ghost of Jock Barefoot. He was in the vicinity of the castle when he spotted a rather fine stick growing from an ancient chestnut tree. Tradition claims that the tree was planted accidentally when a Roman soldier in the vicinity dropped a chestnut from his pocket. In any case, Jock thought that the branch would make a rather fine walking stick for himself. As he was whittling away at it with his knife, Alexander Lindsay, 4th Earl of Crawford, spotted him. The earl was renowned for his ruthlessness, so much so that he was known as 'The Tiger'. He ordered his men to capture Jock and hang him from the chestnut tree as a warning of what would happen to others if they stole things belonging to him.

A few miles east of Finavon stands Kinnaird Castle, a massive pile that is still occupied by the Earls of Southesk. According to local tradition, the 2nd Earl, James Carnegie, was a worshipper of the devil. He studied at Padua University in Northern Italy where he first discovered the art of black magic, and thereafter he fell into league with the devil. It was said that the devil himself taught the most advanced class in the Black Arts, and that Carnegie was one of his pupils. Accordingly, from that time on, the locals claimed that his body cast no shadow, even on the brightest days, which was regarded as a sure sign of his immorality. To prevent others from discovering this, tradition claims that he walked in the shadows from that day onward.

When Carnegie died in 1669 some folk say that a black coach pulled by six dark horses was seen driving through the extensive policies. It was claimed that the coach was ridden by the devil himself, and that he was here to collect the soul of the Earl of Southesk. With the corpse safely on board, the coach and horses rode at breakneck speed away from the castle, and disappeared into a well that is located near to the family burial ground. The sight of the ghostly coach pulled by phantom horses is reputed to take place on nights when the wind howls and the rain lashes through the trees.

The former county of Kincardine was centred on the east-coast town of Stonehaven, but it is now incorporated in a redrawn Aberdeenshire. There are two castles in the immediate vicinity of Stonehaven that are haunted. The first of these, Dunnottar Castle, is regularly open to the public. From the car park by the roadside, a steep path drops down to a narrow spit of land between two bays, before climbing up a gully that leads through gatehouses and on to the headland that the castle occupies. The ruins are extensive, and one can readily appreciate why the castle was virtually impregnable.

Dunnottar is home to a variety of spirits. They have been witnessed at various points in the extensive castle by a number of visitors over the years. One of these ghosts manifested as a tall, fair-haired man of Scandinavian appearance. The witness watched as he made his way up the pathway into the castle. He turned into the guardroom, but when the witness arrived there he discovered that there was no one to be seen.

Another manifestation at Dunnottar appears in the form of a young girl, probably in her early teens. She was seen in the building that was the castle's brewery, and witnesses describe her as being dressed in a dull brown dress. On one occasion the witness gazed in awe as the girl made her way from the doorway at the brewery, turning away from where the onlooker stood. Within a hundred yards or so the spirit disappeared.

One of the vaults in the castle is known as the Covenanters' Prison, for in the seventeenth century 167 supporters of the National Covenant were imprisoned here. There was a lack of space, light and sanitation, and nine of the prisoners died, some by trying to escape down the cliffs. The vault has had a reputation for being haunted since that time.

Other inexplicable things have taken place at Dunnottar. Benholm's Lodging is the name of a building within the castle. On a few occasions visitors have heard the sound of a heated discussion within it, as though some form of meeting were taking place. A little apprehensive at entering the building, in case they disturbed the conversation, they were astounded to discover that the room was totally empty. Another strange spirit at Dunnottar takes the form of a large thin dog like a deerhound. This has been seen at the vaulted tunnel on the entrance pathway and, like other spirits here, it seems to disappear after a short while.

Fetteresso Castle stands a couple of miles to the west of Stonehaven, lying in the valley of the Carron Water. The castle fell into ruins for a short time, losing its roof, but in recent years it has been restored and divided into flats. The Keith family built it in the seventeenth century but it occupies the site of a much older castle that dates from the fifteenth century. Fetteresso is home to a Green Lady. This spirit is usually witnessed on the castle's staircase, and some folk claim that when they saw her they also heard the faint sound of her dress rubbing against the furniture and balustrade. Some of those who have seen the ghost claim that she was carrying a young child at the time. The Green Lady makes her way up the stairs, turning at an angle and disappearing through a stone-built wall. This seemed strange until later investigations revealed that there was a built-up doorway behind the present plaster-work. One of the rooms in the castle is now known as the 'Green Lady's Room'.

Residents at Fetteresso have also reported strange sounds. Some of these are footsteps, probably made by the Green Lady. Maurice and Geraldine Simpson, owners of the castle at one time, heard footsteps and the scraping sound of something being dragged along the basement corridor. The sound was rather metallic, but investigations into its origin proved fruitless. They were later to discover that King Malcolm I was killed nearby, and it has been speculated that the sound heard was the monarch being dragged into the castle, still wearing his armour.

The House of Monymusk is really an ancient castle that stands by the side of the River Don, near to Monymusk village, which lies south-west of the Aberdeenshire town of Inverurie. There is more than one ghost here, the most commonly sighted being the Grey Lady. She seems to have an affinity with young children for she manifests in the nursery. Those who have sighted her state that she appeared from a cupboard within the room.

The second Monymusk ghost has been nicknamed the 'Party Ghost', for he appears when there is a large crowd gathered in the house for a party or other function. As the guests are in the midst of enjoying themselves, one or two are suddenly jolted as if someone has pushed his way through the group. Those who have seen this spectre describe it as being male, wearing a kilt and jacket, with a white-laced shirt.

The library at Monymusk is home to a third spirit. A male figure appears at times, usually seated in a chair reading one of the books. Anyone brave enough to approach the man has discovered that the manifestation disappears before their very eyes. There have been a number of other strange occurrences at Monymusk, from footsteps on the principal stairs when no one is around, to the sound of cavorting in some of the apartments.

Tolquhon Castle is a rather grand ruin of a building, standing in the middle of Aberdeenshire countryside, a few miles from the village of Pitmedden. The castle is protected by Historic Scotland and is regularly open to the public. Here, visitors and locals have seen many sightings of a spirit. It is claimed that a Grey Lady manifests around midnight in the ruins, and can sometimes be seen wandering around the building. She is sometimes heard groaning as if in pain or with grief. There seems to be a different spirit in the castle that appears during the day. Around twenty visitors have reported seeing a slim woman wearing a long dress standing at the top of an old spiral staircase. She never seems to move, preferring to stand staring at visitors. Some of them who have witnessed her have been moved to tears.

Lynn Laughton, one of the custodians at Tolquhon, has experienced a number of inexplicable things during her time there. On a number of occasions she has heard the sound of phantom footsteps making their way up the castle stairs, even though she knows there is no one there to make them. On other occasions she has heard the sound of humming when she is alone.

Lynn lives in a fifteenth-century cottage that stands adjacent to the castle. The cottage seems to be haunted also, for many times she and her family have heard the sound of banging at the kitchen window. This looks over the grounds of the castle. The banging usually occurs at night, and seems to get louder and louder as time goes on. Lynn describes the sound as being like someone knocking at the window as though they are desperate to get in. On investigation nothing or no one to explain the sound is ever seen. Whether or not the Grey Lady or some other spirit is responsible cannot be ascertained.

Kinnaird Head Castle stands on a coastal

headland in the Aberdeenshire town of Fraserburgh. The castle dates from the fifteenth century, but in 1787, when a lighthouse was proposed for Fraserburgh, it was decided to utilize the tower as part of the structure. The light was used from then until 1903, when a paraffin-operated lighthouse replaced it. Since 1995 the lighthouse has formed part of Scotland's Lighthouse Museum, and is maintained by Historic Scotland and the Kinnaird Head Trust.

Most of Kinnaird's surrounding buildings were demolished when the castle was adopted as a lighthouse, but a second tower, known as the Wine Tower, still stands. It is located slightly to the east of the main tower. In the late sixteenth century Sir Alexander Fraser of Philorth owned the tower. It was he who established the harbour and town of Fraserburgh, but he bankrupted himself and had to sell most of his estates in 1611. He had a daughter, Isobel, who fell in love with a man Fraser thought was not good enough for her. Despite his protestations she insisted that she carry on with the romance. Sir Alexander was eventually forced into drastic action. He captured the lover and dragged him to a cave that existed beneath the Wine Tower. He was tied up there and left to face the incoming tide. Sir Alexander had planned simply to frighten the beau, and release him, but he miscalculated the tides and the unfortunate man drowned.

Isobel discovered what her father had done and ran to the tower, only to find her lover's lifeless body. In a fit of depression she lunged from the tower, killing herself when she landed on the rocks below. It is said that the ghost of Isobel appears in the vicinity of the Wine Tower whenever there is a wild storm, as though she is searching for her lover.

Rothiemay Castle in Banffshire has been demolished and replaced by a smaller country house on the same site. The castle seems to have been home to three different spectres. The ghost of Lt.-Col. J. Foster Forbes, who died in 1914, was witnessed a number of times by his grandchildren long after he had died. Even those who had never met him reported seeing his spirit, later confirmed by referring to photographs. A portrait was used to identify a female spirit that manifested in the castle's vaulted dining-room. Violet Tweedale spotted an old lady sitting near to the fireplace. She was wearing a plaid shawl, but after a short while the ghost faded away. She described what she had seen to members of the Forbes family, but no one knew who she could be until a portrait depicting the former owners (the

Duff family) was studied — the old lady appeared in it.

One of the Forbes ladies was once in her room when she became aware of a presence in the hall outside. A figure seemed to be slowly shuffling along the passage, holding on to the wainscoting to feel the way. Slightly frightened, the lady was able to ask, 'Is that you?' thinking it was her brother. However, the shuffling stopped and a loud thump was heard in the corridor. When she went to investigate there was nothing to be seen.

A similar experience occurred when a woman heard the sound of loud arguing emanating from the Morning Room. She listened to this for some time before deciding to enter the room and find out what the cause of the argument was. As she opened the door she was astonished to discover that the room was totally dark and empty.

A number of old accounts of Rothiemay castle claim that a room known as Queen Mary's Room was haunted. The spirit witnessed here was not of Mary Queen of Scots but of children. They seemed to be crying in a corner of the room. Revd Henry Brett, a chaplain from Eastbourne, stayed in this room on a number of occasions. On two separate nights he heard the crying. On the third night when the sobbing started he rose from his bed, donned his robes once more and lit some candles. He then read prayers of exorcism after which the crying was never heard again.

Cromarty Castle has not existed for many years. Originally dating from the thirteenth century or earlier, it was eventually demolished in the second half of the seventeenth century when Cromarty House was erected as a more comfortable replacement. The castle stood in the small village of Cromarty, which stands on a promontory projecting into the Cromarty Firth. When the castle was still standing, the occupants often heard strange noises within it. These were extremely variable in character, and ranged from groans and moans, to screams and footsteps. Some of the residents in the castle are also said to have seen various ghosts, but as the castle was demolished so long ago, accounts of what they experienced have long since been forgotten.

When Cromarty Castle was being dismantled the workmen discovered a strange secret which was not known about, or even recorded in legend. Built into one of the walls was a large quantity of human bones, and it was significant that many of the skeletons were missing their heads. Whether or not the bones had anything to do with the ghosts of

Cromarty cannot be determined, as no explanation for them has ever been forthcoming.

Argyll has a number of haunted castles within its confines. Barcaldine Castle was another of Sir Duncan Campbell of Glenorchy's structures. It was erected in the late sixteenth century at the western end of his extensive estates. Today it is home to Roderick Campbell, Younger of Barcaldine, and the attractive tower is open to the public. Barcaldine Castle was an integral part of the Massacre of Glencoe. It was here that MacIan of Glencoe was detained for twenty-four hours in a plot to prevent him from swearing the oath of allegiance to William III in the given time, which would have prevented the massacre from taking place.

The ghost at Barcaldine has nothing to do with the massacre, however. In the Argyll Room guests have reported seeing a manifestation of a female figure, known as the Blue Lady. The ghost is often seen playing the piano in the room, and usually the sound of playing can be heard, even though no one is touching the instrument at the time. It has been remarked that the sound of the piano is most often heard on windy nights. For the benefit of tourists visiting the castle, the

Argyll Room has an upright piano at which a dummy representing the ghost is seated.

The original of the Blue Lady is thought to be Harriet Campbell, daughter of Sir Alexander Campbell, 2nd Baronet. She never married and lived in the nineteenth and early twentieth centuries, when the castle was restored and re-roofed by her brother, Sir Duncan. Photographs of her survive, and her appearance matches exactly to descriptions of the spirit in the castle.

On the opposite side of Ardmucknish Bay from Barcaldine stands Dunstaffnage Castle, a magnificent ruin perched on top of a solid rock boss. This castle is one of the oldest stone buildings in Scotland, with records existing of a fortification here as early as the seventh century. The castle passed into Campbell hands and today the ruin is protected by Historic Scotland and is regularly open to the public.

Visitors may hear the strange sounds that have been reported over the centuries. Dunstaffnage seems to be the home of some form of invisible spirit that makes strange noises. These can take the form of footsteps, thuds and various other types of loud noises. As always, there is never any form of earthly reason behind the noise.

When the castle was still occupied by the

Campbell family, the children used to complain of an unknown thing that would annoy them in their beds. Their parents put this down to the children preferring to stay up late, but the strange noises occurred over such a long period of time, and with different generations of children that there was thought to be more in it. The children often stated that the ghost teased them in some way or other, and that they heard loud noises. On a number of occasions it was even claimed that the room itself shook, as though an earthquake had taken place.

Dunstaffnage is one of a number of castles that have spirits that manifest to herald a death in the family. Here the spirit is female in form, usually dressed in green, and is known as the 'Ell-maid of Dunstaffnage'. A few accounts name the ghost as the Green Lady, whereas those in Gaelic name her the *Scannag*. When the Ell-maid appears with a tear-strewn expression, then the family knows to expect a death in the not too distant future. The Ell-maid was unique in some respects in that she could also appear with a smiling face. This was to be interpreted as good news for the family, which may include a birth or wedding ceremony.

In Gaelic folklore the heralds of death are known as *gruagach*, which translates as 'a household goddess or brownie'.

In the Firth of Clyde is the island of Bute, the principal town of which is Rothesay. The castle here was an important structure in its day, and still occupies an island site surrounded by a moat. Being a royal castle (the heir to the throne is the Duke of Rothesay) the building has a hereditary keeper in the Marquess of Bute.

In 1230 Viking raiders captured Rothesay Castle. They managed to gain entry by constructing a shelter that was placed against an external wall. The Vikings worked away within this, hacking at the stone with axes and adzes. On entering the courtyard the occupants of the castle were all put to death by the Norsemen, apart from one of the daughters, a Lady Isobel. She was a young and attractive woman, and one of the Vikings decided that she would make him an ideal wife. Lady Isobel was for none of this, however. She escaped to a stairway located between the circular perimeter wall and the gable of the chapel. This originally gave access to the first floor of the building. On the stairway Lady Isobel withdrew a dagger and plunged it into her body a number of times, killing herself. Since that time the stairway has been known as the 'Bloody Stair'.

The Hebrides off the west coast of

Scotland are home to a number of ancient castles that are haunted by various spectres. Caisteal Chamuis on the island of Skye is today a strange ruin located on a cliff-top, three miles or so north of Armadale. The MacLeods built the castle, but it passed to the MacDonalds and was finally abandoned about 1689. Another *gruagach* was said to haunt this building when it was still complete. As with the one at Dunstaffnage, this spirit appeared before both good and bad times. Here also a *glaislig*, or fairy, was said to appear at night, when everyone was asleep, and do some chores for the family. The night-time spirit of Caisteal Chamuis was said to particularly care for the cattle.

South of Skye are the Small Isles, which comprise the islands of Muck, Rum, Canna and Eigg. On the island of Canna are the fragmentary ruins of Coroghan Castle, occupying a cliff-top location. The castle has a long and bloody history. In the seventeenth century (perhaps in 1666) Donald Mac-Donald of Clanranald imprisoned a woman, possibly his wife, here. Her spirit reputedly haunts the ruins.

6

Holy Spirits

Many ghosts prefer to haunt sites associated with religion. There are a number of old abbeys and churchyards that are said to be haunted, as well as places more loosely associated with worship.

Monks have been reported as manifesting in a number of places, some of which will be mentioned elsewhere in this book. In Aberdeen there have been many reported sightings of monks appearing in the vicinity of Carmelite Street. As can be gathered from the street name, this was at one time the site of a monastery of the Carmelite friars. It was established around 1273 but was ransacked and subsequently demolished at the time of the Reformation. Nothing now remains of the friary apart from the street name and the spirit of a friar that has appeared a number of times. A local publican witnessed an unusual presence in the bar that he put down to the spirit of the friary, and the ghost also visited a neighbouring shop. Most of these occurrences took place when the site of the friary was being excavated prior to some redevelopment work.

In the same city St Nicholas' Church stands off Union Street on a site that has been used for worship since at least the twelfth century. The graveyard here has a long history of hauntings, and spirits have been reported right up to modern times. One of the most recent incidents took place in 1982. Two men were in the graveyard when they became aware of a woman dressed in a long white dress. Over her head was a veil, making her look rather like a bride. However, as the men watched her walking through the graveyard, they suddenly discovered that she was not a bride of the present when the apparition disappeared next to the ancient church building.

The Revd Spencer Nairne was walking along the street with a friend of his, John Chambers, in the early summer of 1859. They were heading for the city's harbour in order to board a ship bound for Norway. As he made his way down the street the minister spotted a friend of his, Miss Wallis, coming in the opposite direction. She had been a friend of the family ever since she had worked as a governess on their behalf. The two people walked ever closer towards each other, and as they neared Miss Wallis smiled at the minister. However, just as he was about to speak to her he was struck dumb as she disappeared before his very eyes. When he came to his senses he looked round to see if he had mistakenly missed her stepping aside or something, but there was no sign of her.

Spencer Nairne continued on his way and paid his visit to Norway. When he returned he was called down to London on business. By chance he met Miss Wallis there, and she was busy talking to some of his family. As he appeared she spoke to him, scolding him lightly for ignoring her as she walked past him in the street. The minister explained that he had seen her coming towards him, but just as he was about to speak she disappeared completely. Miss Wallis was aghast at this, for she had experienced the same thing! She had been walking down the street and was about to talk to Revd Nairne when he vanished in front of her.

On another day the minister and Miss Wallis were discussing their strange encounter. As they talked they became aware of the fact that they seemed to be referring to different days. Miss Wallis placed the incident towards the end of July, whereas Nairne knew it was the 31 May from his departure date. It was concluded that their strange experience could only be explained by them having passed through some form of 'time slip'. These occur when someone witnesses an event that took place at a different time to that in which they are actually living. The slip may only be a few weeks apart, as in the case of Spencer Nairne, but in other examples witnesses have experienced battles re-enacting in front of them or other sights that could only come from a different decade or century.

Today Deer Abbey is but a fragmentary ruin standing in the fertile Buchan countryside, eleven miles west of Peterhead. The abbey was erected around 1219 but was abandoned shortly after the Reformation, and has since fallen into ruin. The ruins are now protected as an ancient monument by Historic Scotland. A number of tales associate the abbey with a ghostly monk. This figure has been reported a number of times over the years. On some occasions he has wandered as far as the nearby road, causing traffic to swerve to avoid him. Those who have seen this spectre describe it as sporting a dark coloured robe. Although a hood covers the head, witnesses state that the face is only visible as a blur, as if they are seeing it out of focus.

There seem to be very few haunted churches in Scotland. Perhaps as Christians often regard ghosts and spectres as 'evil spirits', they tend not to frequent holy buildings. One church that is haunted, however, has in recent years been converted into a theatre. St David's Ramshorn church stands right in the centre of the city of Glasgow. Despite being a tall structure, itself and its graveyard are somewhat dwarfed by the surrounding buildings. Shortly after the building was converted to the Ramshorn Theatre people began to notice that the toilets were haunted by a female spectre. This manifestation was given the name Edie, although who she may have been in life is a mystery. Any sighting of her is accompanied by a strong smell, and on some occasions footsteps have been heard. The toilets occupy what had formerly been the minister's vestry, and beneath the floor is an ancient vault which some say has a connection with the haunting.

General Sir David Leslie (or Lord Newark as he became) has already been mentioned in connection with Newark Castle in Fife. Whereas the castle is haunted by the General's daughter, the Auld Kirk at St Monans is haunted by his spectre. One evening sometime in the early twentieth century, the beadle of the kirk was busily cleaning out the boiler after the fire had burned itself out. He had gathered all the ashes into a steel bucket and was in the process of carrying it towards the kirkyard dike, in order to throw them into the water, when something caught his attention out of the corner of his eye. He turned and looked up at the church steeple and was aghast to notice a face gazing down from one of the openings in it. The beadle, who knew the kirk inside out, thought that he was the only person in the building at the time; in addition to this, in order to reach the opening from where the figure was looking one would have required a ladder or scaffolding.

The beadle, having convinced himself that there was no one in the kirk, and that he must have been dreaming, put the vision to the back of his mind. However, within a short time he had cause to visit the manse of Abercrombie. Within the building was a copy of an old portrait of Sir David Leslie that had been painted by George Jameson. The colour in the beadle's face drained when he saw the picture, for it was the exact image of the face he had seen gazing from the tower.

Hobkirk church stands remotely in Roxburghshire, one of the former Border counties. The present church was erected in the nineteenth century by the side of the Rule Water, seven miles south-east of Hawick, but it replaced an older building, the only vestiges of which are visible as low mounds of earth in the kirkyard. The Revd Nicol Edgar was appointed minister of this older church in 1694. By 1720 he had served the parish for twenty-six years, and was by then sixty-two years of age. That year the people of the parish began to report sightings of a ghost within the old kirkyard. He was described as a tall man, wearing a blue bonnet. Some even claimed that he had manifested within the church itself. The stories associated with the ghost grew to such an extent that eventually even Edgar's daughters refused to go out at night, frightened in case they witnessed the spectre.

Nicol Edgar decided that he would have to do something about the ghost. He took one of the large black bibles from the church and an old claymore that had been handed down in his family. With them he ventured to the kirkyard in the gloaming, and there he waited for darkness. Using the claymore he drew a circle around himself on the ground, a traditional method of keeping evil spirits at bay. He then sat down and held the Bible open.

The minister remained there all night, seeing nothing that resembled a ghost. However, just as morning was beginning to break, he became aware of the ghost arising

132

out of the ground. The spirit made its way towards the minister, but stopped short of the circle on the ground. He removed his blue socks and threw them over the mark on the ground, into the circle. The minister lifted them up, and was amazed to discover that they were typical woollen stockings, not ghostly in any way. With growing courage, the minister asked the ghost why it kept appearing in the area.

'I was a cattle dealer in the Borders,' replied the spectre, 'but one Lammas whilst I was returning home from the fair I was robbed and murdered. My corpse was hidden on the moors. Since that time my spirit has been restless, and until I get a proper burial in the kirkyard it will wander the parish.'

Nicol Edgar arranged for a search party and, true enough, they found the body of the murdered man. It was taken to Hobkirk and buried in the churchyard, since which time there have been no sightings of the spectre.

In the Kincardineshire town of Banchory a monk has manifested a number of times in recent years. He seems to keep to the older part of the expanding town, appearing at odd times. The monk is probably associated with an ancient monastery that stood here, founded around 430 AD by St Ternan.

Newbattle Abbey is home to another

strange spirit that haunts the older parts of the building. David I founded the abbey in 1140 but during the Reformation it was secularized by the Kerrs. Most of the abbey was demolished and rebuilt as a country house, although the vaulted undercrofts survive to give some indication of what it was once like. The building is now used as a college. No one has really witnessed a ghost in the building, but many people claim that some sort of evil spirit has made them feel uncomfortable. Very few people are willing to stay in the building after nightfall.

The Dryburgh Abbey Hotel has already been mentioned in chapter three. It was named after the ancient abbey that stands in ruins nearby, also cared for by Historic Scotland. As with most abbey hauntings, the ghosts seen by witnesses appear as monks. They have been witnessed a number of times by visitors over the years, sometimes singly and at other times in a group.

Old graveyards are ideal spots for ghosts to appear. Although spirits are usually associated with places they frequented in life, many seem to prefer to haunt the quiet kirkyard where they were laid to rest. One of the most haunted kirkyards in Scotland seems to be Greyfriars in Edinburgh. The burial ground is one of the oldest in the city, and is located on the southern side of the Old Town. A number of 'Ghost Tours' that explore the city make it one of their ports of call.

Buried in Greyfriars is Sir George MacKenzie of Rosehaugh (1636–91), who was the Lord Advocate for Scotland in the second half of the seventeenth century. He was responsible for sentencing many Covenanters to death, and as a result his opponents knew him as 'Bluidy MacKenzie'. For some reason his ghost seems to be one of the most active in the kirkyard, and many folk claim that it is responsible for physical harm experienced by them. Many visitors to the kirkyard experience some form of pain for which they can see no apparent reason. When they touch the part that aches they discover blood has been shed, and when they next look in a mirror they are shocked to find that their face, arms or uncovered legs have scratch marks on them.

'Bluidy MacKenzie' does not keep his appearances to the kirkyard. His ghost also haunts a public house in nearby Niddry Street. A number of regulars there have seen him at various times. Some of the haunting incidents in the city's Niddry Street vaults are also attributed to Mackenzie. Visitors to these vaults have experienced many strange things. A young boy of eleven years old was in the vault when he felt his forehead being brushed by what he thought was a cobweb. The sensation quickly passed, but on leaving the vaults he discovered that there were three scratches above his eyebrows. Some folk reckon that MacKenzie has been responsible for around one hundred paranormal activities over the last century, but it has been claimed that he is making many more appearances in recent years.

A psychic, Ruth Urquhart, visited the graveyard in 2000 and was shocked when the spirit seemed to attack her. It clawed at the sleeves of her jacket and at her scarf, leaving them torn to shreds. Ruth claims that it left her in considerable pain. Nevertheless, she claimed that the spirit was a friendly one, and that it was only trying to direct her to the burial vault of Bluidy MacKenzie. In her trance she was able to see the corpses of many Covenanters lying on the ground, many of them starved to death. Ruth was able to contact the spirit of one of the martyrs, William MacKenzie of Edinburgh, who had been held in the Covenanters' Prison.

Many other visitors to the graveyard have experienced strange psychic happenings. On a number of occasions visitors have been pushed to the ground by unseen forces.

Amanda Hamilton of Portobello was taking a tour through the churchyard when she discovered that she was unable to speak. She felt as though she was being suffocated and soon passed out. The Revd Colin Grant, a spiritualist minister, tried to exorcize the churchyard using a Bible and crucifix. This took two attempts, for on the first he was too frightened to pass through the churchyard gates. He was able to enter the kirkyard on the second attempt, but made no contact with MacKenzie. Grant was to die shortly afterwards.

The old kirkyard of Blairgowrie is located at the north end of the town, overlooking the River Ericht. A tale from 1730 associates the burial ground with the ghost of Mause. William Soutar was a crofter who lived near to Bridge of Cally, which lies five miles to the north-west. For some time a large black dog that seemed to follow him everywhere had pestered him, and as soon as he managed to lose it, it appeared from the opposite direction. From its ability to do this, and because of traditional beliefs, he knew that it was the spectre of a murderer. It was said that his spirit could not lie at peace until the corpse of his victim was given a decent Christian burial.

William Soutar followed the dog one day.

The animal seemed to be calmer now that it had his attention, and it led him to a quiet spot in the countryside. Soutar dug down a few inches and soon came across the bones of the murdered man. Now that the corpse had been discovered it was lifted and taken to Blairgowrie where it was laid to rest in the churchyard. From that time on the ghost of Mause was never seen again — or so they say.

The former manse of Methlick in Aberdeenshire is now the Gight House Hotel. Guests here have witnessed a number of strange sights over the years, as well as hearing noises coming from empty rooms. The sound of footsteps has been heard emanating from unoccupied rooms, and on one occasion a bathroom door was locked from the inside when no one was there. Sightings of the building's ghost are rarer. Those who have seen the spectre reckon that it is the manifestation of the Revd John Mennie, who occupied the manse until his death in 1886. He has appeared in various rooms throughout the house, including bedrooms and the room now converted into the hotel bar.

The present Kinross manse was erected in 1769, making it one of the oldest buildings in the historical town. It has long had a reputation for being haunted. It is said that on occasion the minister, or another member of his family, has been sitting in one of the rooms and heard the sound of footsteps walking across the floor of the room overhead. Knowing that they should have been the only person present in the manse, they rather apprehensively scaled the stairs and pushed the door open slowly, frightened of what they might find. However, once the door was fully ajar the room was discovered to be empty.

On other occasions the minister in Kinross manse has awoken in the middle of the night to the sound of a baby crying. Again the sound seemed to come from another room, but when he wandered through the house to find the source of the noise, he discovered that there was nothing to be found.

The previous manse building at Kinross also had a reputation for being haunted. In 1718 a Mr Sinclair published an article entitled 'Endorism, or a strange relation of dreams or spirits that troubled the minister's house of Kinross'. The minister at that time was the Revd Robert MacGill, who served from 1699 until 1719. He discovered that silver cutlery mysteriously disappeared from the house, only to turn up later in the barn. On one occasion, a cupboard that had hung on the wall for many years suddenly dropped to the ground, breaking all the dishes within it. For a period of time pins and small needles turned up regularly within meat and boiled eggs. MacGill's wife decided to supervise the cook one day, to make sure that she was not putting pins in the food to try and harm the minister. Despite the utmost security, she too was astonished to find that the dish prepared was full of small pins.

Often, when clothing or bed linen was hung out to dry, the maid would go out to bring it in only to find that it had been ripped to shreds. Clothing that had been left in cupboards was later discovered to be torn in half, damaged beyond repair. Even visitors to the house discovered that the clothes in which they stood developed small tears for no apparent reason.

All of these disturbances were thought to be the work of a servant girl in the manse. She was suspected of trying to steal the silverware by hiding it in the barn, in order to collect it later. However, there was never any proof forthcoming to convict her. The strange disturbances were eventually put down to some form of poltergeist activity.

Things gradually became more serious. On one occasion the minister's very own Bible was suddenly forced into the air and landed in the middle of the fire. The minister rushed to grab a poker and rake it out. Once he was satisfied that it was cool enough to touch he found to his amazement that the Bible was totally unmarked. On another day, however, when silver cutlery was launched into the fire, it melted into blobs of metal.

The strange happenings at Kinross manse suddenly stopped just as quickly as they had started, and apart from the weird sounds in the present building, there have been no more reports of poltergeists at work.

A third manse, located at Strachur in Argyll, also has a reputation for being haunted. On one occasion an army captain called at the manse where he stayed overnight with his relatives. He spent some time catching up on the family gossip before going to bed. As he lay there the curtains round his four-poster bed gradually opened to reveal a face. The captain was unperturbed by this, thinking that one of the family was unaware that he was there. However, the curtains opened three times to reveal the same face. By this time the captain was getting rather annoyed at the constant disruption, so he asked the person what he wanted.

'I come with some information. One year from this night you will meet your father,' it responded.

The captain was more concerned now. His

father had died some time ago, and he could not work out what the person had meant. The next morning, after a restless sleep, he went down to breakfast and related what he had seen to his hosts. They could not explain the vision either, for up until that time there was no evidence of the manse having been haunted.

However, exactly one year later the captain was back at the manse. He was heading north on business, but called in at the manse *en route*. Having enjoyed tea with his relatives he told them that he must proceed, for he had business to attend to. They pleaded with him to stay, for the weather was wild and they reckoned that the ferry across Loch Fyne to Inveraray would be cancelled. They were right, but the captain flew into a rage and forced the ferryman and his son to take the boat out. They rowed the captain, his servant and horse out into the stormy waters, but halfway across decided that it was too rough and windy to try and force their way any further. They decided to return.

As the boat was being manoeuvred for its return back to the port it capsized. All were still alive, and the captain told the servant, who could not swim, to hold on to the horse. The other three tried to swim for the shore. The ferryman, who was older, was too frail to make it and he drowned within a short distance. The son was stronger but he too succumbed in the waters. The captain managed to reach the shore, but by that time he was suffering from pneumonia and so exhausted that he died on the beach. Only the servant lad survived, dragged ashore by the horse.

A former archbishop of St Andrews haunts Melgund Castle in Angus. Cardinal David Beaton held the archbishopric from 1539 until 29 May 1546 when he was murdered in St Andrews Castle. His lifeless corpse was then hung naked from the battlements. Melgund was Beaton's own property, for he built the castle in the sixteenth century and Marion Ogilvie, his lawfully relinquished wife who he continued to meet as a mistress, lived there for a time. Since his death his restless spirit has haunted the castle, even though it was in ruins for many years. The building was restored in recent years and occupied once more as a family home. Whether or not the spirit of the archbishop still haunts the building cannot yet be ascertained.

Cardinal Beaton's ghost has also been reported at another Angus castle. Ethie Castle stands in open countryside five miles to the north-east of Arbroath. The Cardinal also commissioned this building, and his spirit is most often seen in the 'secret passage'. More information on the haunting of Ethie can be found in the author's previous book, *Scottish Ghosts*.

Spynie Castle is sometimes known as Spynie Palace, as it was the Bishop of Moray's palace. The extensive ruins are indistinguishable from a true fortified castle, however, and following a number of years of consolidation work, are now open to the public under the auspices of Historic Scotland. The great tower dates from the fifteenth century. Within its thick walls some folk have heard the phantom sound of a piper playing. A few folk claim to have witnessed the spectre making his way along one of the corridors.

Spynie has a second spectral presence in its ruins. The ghost of a lion traditionally haunts the great tower, known as Davy's Tower after Bishop David Stewart who built it between 1462 and 1477. Reports of sightings have also been made in the ruinous kitchen wing of the castle, which was built immediately to the north of the tower. Tradition claims that one of the bishops kept a lion as a pet, and that the animal's spirit has frightened unsuspecting visitors since that time.

7

Haunted Homes

Haunted buildings need not be large and imposing castles, or particularly ancient either. Many smaller homes are haunted — typical everyday buildings that could be located in your street or mine. The hauntings that take place in these buildings are usually of spirits that have no known provenance, they are manifestations of people who just happened to live there, or else lived in a building that formerly occupied the same site.

The author has spoken to many people who have experienced some sort of paranormal activity in their own home. In most cases the witness was not frightened to any great extent, rather they just experienced the sight of some form of spirit or other, usually in a calm and ordered way. In a number of other cases, however, the spirit in the house has frightened the occupier so much that they decide instantly that they need to move elsewhere.

There are numerous haunted houses in the city of Edinburgh. Heriot Row is located in the city's New Town and was developed between 1802–8. New owners purchased one of the upmarket houses overlooking Queen Street Gardens in 1981 and suddenly discovered that it was haunted. At night they would close the internal wooden shutters before retiring to bed. Next morning they would awake to the sight of the sun streaming through the open shutters. The owners thought that perhaps it was the wind that caused the shutters to open, but they were capable of doing this even on the calmest of nights. Eventually they resorted to placing a heavy pot plant on the windowsill to keep the shutters closed. On any occasion that they forgot to do this, the shutters were able to open by themselves.

The new owners decided to do some alterations to the house, and when the the work was under way they discovered a secret compartment of which they had no previous knowledge. When this room was entered, strange sounds emanated throughout the building before subsiding to an eerie silence.

Another thing that the owners of the Heriot Row house could not explain was the large trunk that they found in the attic of the house. It was a substantial box, manufactured from solid teak, and was in the house when they bought it. However, on closer inspection they discovered that there was a label on the trunk, and the address on the label matched the house in Heriot Row. They were able to ascertain that the trunk had been sent from Sri Lanka. What totally unnerved the owners was the fact that the name on the label was their own, and that it was dated before they had acquired the house. It was as if some unknown spirit had sent the trunk to the house, knowing that the family would later live there.

A house in Royal Circus (which lies just to the north of Heriot Row) was being divided into flats by developers in 1973. They employed workmen to carry out the renovations, but were taken aback when they threatened to go on strike as a result of the house's ghost. Just as the work was starting one of the workmen spotted a young woman wandering through the building. She was wearing a long white dress and passed from room to room. The workman thought that she was just a nosy passer by, having a look at the building whilst it was empty. However, he saw her again, and within days many of the other workers were talking about the same woman. They decided that they would have to talk to her, and explain that she could not just come in off the street at will, for the building was not only private, the work meant that it was also dangerous at the time. Each time she was seen thereafter, however, the workmen could never quite catch her — she would nip into the other room and by the time the worker had laid down his tools and followed her she had gone.

Things came to a head one day when three workmen spotted her and followed her into a room. Ready to have it out with her over her trespassing, they were left standing in trepidation when she disappeared before their very eyes. When they were able to pull themselves back together they decided that they would have to consult their union and perhaps go on strike. After some negotiation the developers agreed to let a psychic medium investigate. She went into the house and wandered from room to room. She then came back outside and was able to report to the workers that she was a friendly spirit and would do them no harm. With some reassurance the builders went back to work, and were happy to report that no other sightings of the woman were made again.

A house in Jamaica Street (which lies midway between Heriot Row and Royal Circus) was reputedly haunted by a figure of a man. He had a decidedly pale complexion, but the bright red hat that he wore brightened up his manifestation. His spirit regularly appeared in the late eighteenth and early nineteenth centuries. It has even been claimed that on the odd occasion the spirit would talk to James Campbell, who was the tenant of the house. Campbell was not scared of the spirit, and began to let others know of the unexpected guest in his house. Word of his gossip reached the owner of the building, who reckoned that the tenant was spreading rumours of the haunting in order to keep down the rents in the building. The landlord took Campbell to court in 1815, to try and have him silenced. However, Campbell was adamant that he did see the spirit of the man, and even called a few witnesses to back up his story. The court was unimpressed with his tale, and actually fined him £5, which was a considerable sum of money to him. He was also ordered never to mention the ghostly happenings in Jamaica Street again. Cheekily, James Campbell asked the judge on leaving if he would still be allowed to talk to the ghost!

A house in Buckingham Terrace (in the Dean area of the city) is home to the strange spirit of an old sailor. The Gordon family rented the flat for a time, and it was they who seem to have mostly experienced the haunting. The tenement building had offices on the lower two floors, the Gordons' flat on the second floor, and a furniture store on the top level. On a number of occasions Mrs Gordon would be disturbed during her sleep by the sound of bangs and moving furniture coming from above. At first she was not scared by the sound, rather, she was just annoyed at the fact that the storemen always seemed to need to move the furniture during the night. She complained to the landlord about the disturbances during the night, but he assured her that the sound would not be coming from the top floor as the store was rarely used. Instead he advised her that the sound was probably travelling in the silence of the night from another block in the tenement.

Mrs Gordon heard the rumblings and bangs on a number of other occasions, and she was convinced that they did indeed come from the room directly over her bedroom. She was a bit disturbed to discover that her daughters never seemed to hear any of the noises, being able to sleep soundly.

One night, however, Mrs Gordon was absent from the house. One of her daughters, Diana, decided to sleep in her mother's room. That night she awoke to hear rumblings overhead. When she climbed out of bed a strange spirit brushed past her. The apparition headed out of the room and up the stairs, disappearing into the furniture store.

Diana was able to follow it, and she managed to enter the store. There she could see an indistinct shape, almost human in proportion, standing next to an antique grandfather clock. It seemed to be busy working on something within the case, though it did not seem to be winding up the weights.

Mrs Gordon experienced the sounds on another occasion, and she tried to ring a hand bell that she kept by the side of her bed in case of emergencies. As she reached out to grab it, however, she fell from her bed and landed on the floor. One of her fingernails was broken in the fall. As she managed to gather herself together she witnessed a strange shadowy figure similar to that seen by Diana. It passed through the closed door and seemed to head up the stairs. Sounds from the upper floor could be heard for about thirty minutes thereafter.

The Gordons decided that they would have to leave the flat, and were even happy to pay the penalty on their lease for leaving without giving sufficient notice. Research into the history of the house revealed that an old sailor, who was rather too fond of his rum, had occupied it. This, coupled with a short temper, made him a totally unpleasant character. It was claimed that one night he was awakened by the sound of a young child, and in a fit of temper left his bedroom, climbed the stairs and shook it to death. He then tried to hide the corpse in the case of a grandfather clock. The sailor was later arrested for his crime, but he was judged to be insane and was consequently sent to a lunatic asylum. He was later to commit suicide.

Leamington Terrace is a Victorian-style street of well-to-do homes in Edinburgh's Bruntsfield. Although the residents of various homes in the terrace have experienced strange occurrences, no one has actually seen a ghost there. Many of the tenants have felt things pass by them, or else been aware of something in their company. On a few occasions the residents have claimed that they felt the spirit was trying to tell them something, but could not bring itself, or was unable, to do this. Who the spirit may have been in life is not known.

St Mary's Street is located in the oldest part of Edinburgh, striking south from the Royal Mile. The street only dates from 1868, however, for old buildings around the close known as St Mary's Wynd were demolished and the thoroughfare widened. The street was the location of a rather brutal murder in 1916. A young woman was walking along the street when an assailant lunged at her from a passageway. The attacker withdrew his knife and plunged it into her body. No robbery was committed or any apparent motive for the attack ever discovered. The murderer simply ran off into the night. The woman's body was discovered later, lying in a pool of blood. Despite extensive investigations, the murderer was never found. Since that night, however, the spirit of the woman has sometimes been seen in St Mary's Street. Witnesses have reported the figure of a woman standing at the entrance of the passageway from where the attack came. Her clothing is splattered with drops of blood, and she seems to be staring in amazement around her, as though she cannot believe what has happened.

Muirhouse Gardens is a much more modern housing development, erected in the 1950s and 1960s and comprising of blocks of low-rise flats, located between Pilton and Cramond. These were built on an ancient site, and some aged trees were retained when the houses were erected. Many of the residents in this street have witnessed the strange spirit of an old man. He has long tangled hair and his eyes always seem to stare blankly. This ghost usually haunts the open lawns around the houses, flitting from tree to tree, and those who have seen him claim that the feeling they get from him is that he is a particularly evil spectre. Who the man was in life is not known.

Another modern Edinburgh house that was subject to some strange paranormal activities was 47 Stevenson Drive, which is located in the Stenhouse area. Mr and Mrs Michael Rodgers occupied this house, but she died in 1954. Shortly after, some strange writing appeared on the wall of the house. The letters appeared randomly, and no amount of deciphering could work out what was trying to be written. Mr Rodgers reckoned that this was his wife trying to contact him from beyond the grave, but the meaning of what appeared puzzled him also. After a short time the appearance of the writing ceased, and the house no longer seems to have any supernatural connections.

In 1780 George Gourlay and his growing family occupied one of the flats in a tenement located in Edinburgh's Bell's Wynd, which is located off the High Street. He regularly paid his rent to the factor (agent) employed by his landlord, Patrick Guthrie, and as his family grew felt that he could do with some extra space. He was always aware of the empty flat located on the floor beneath his own home, and one day asked the factor if it would be possible for him to rent this also. The landlord steadfastly refused, giving no reason for this decision. Gourlay asked on more than one occasion if he could lease the flat, but he was always given the same answer.

One day Gourlay lost his patience and decided to break into the flat. When he passed through the battered door he discovered that the rooms were still furnished, although they were a bit dusty. As he wandered through the flat he was suddenly shocked when a ghostly female figure appeared to him. Frightened out of his wits, he ran from the building.

Gourlay was so terrified by the ghost that he went to a local procurator fiscal to report his experience. He was convinced that there must be something sinister in the flat because of the ghost and because of Guthrie's refusal to let it. Gourlay was surprised once more when he related his tale to the procurator fiscal — he was charged with breaking and entering! The procurator fiscal, however, went to Bell's Wynd to investigate. As he wandered through the flat he discovered the corpse of a woman lying on the floor. Patrick Guthrie was apprehended and asked to explain why the body was in the flat and what had happened to it. He told the procurator fiscal that he had returned home early one evening only to discover his wife in the arms of another man. Guthrie and the clandestine

155

lover began to brawl, and Guthrie's wife tried to stop them. In the mêlée she was injured so severely that she died shortly thereafter.

The case went further, and although at the time the name of the lover was not released, it was claimed that he was a high-ranking nobleman and should his name become public knowledge then the ensuing scandal would have considerable repercussions. Nevertheless, he did confirm Guthrie's story. The corpse of Mrs Guthrie was later taken and given a Christian burial in a churchyard, but it is claimed that her apparition still occasionally appears in the steep close that is Bell's Wynd.

A similar story explains the haunting of Fountainhall, an eighteenth-century house in Blenheim Place, Aberdeen. The ghost of a female figure has been reported over the years, and some folk claim that it is the spirit of a woman who was murdered by her husband. He had discovered her to be having an affair with another man, and tradition claims that he was a nobleman of some standing. After murdering his wife, the owner of the house hid her body beneath the floor. Since that time the house has been subject to strange knocking sounds, and mysterious footsteps have been heard in different parts of the building. Strange crashing sounds have also been heard, as though items of furniture were being thrown around the room. On further investigation no sign of any disturbance is ever seen. In the late eighteenth and early nineteenth centuries the house was home to Dr Patrick Copland, who died in 1822. He had been a professor of Natural Philosophy at Marischal College in the city, but whether or not it was he who killed his wife is not known.

Another Aberdeen house is home to half a ghost. Devanha House was erected in 1813 just off Holbourn Street, in the Ferryhill district of the city. The building probably suffered a fire within twenty or thirty years of being built, for it is known that it was rebuilt and extended in 1840 to the plans of the noted Aberdeenshire architect, Archibald Simpson. The spirit that haunts the house appears as the upper half of an old woman. She only appears from the waist up and is distinguished by her straggly grey hair. She wears a white nightgown that hangs down loosely from her torso. Various sightings of the spirit have been reported, even up to modern times, for the building is now occupied by a company connected with the oil industry. The fact that she appears only from the waist up might be attributed to the fact that the floor levels of the house have probably changed, a phenomenon that has been reported elsewhere.

Carol Cowie lives on a farm in Gamrie parish, Banffshire, but she remembers witnessing a ghost in her parents' house, a modern bungalow that stands in Corskie Place, in the fishing town of Macduff in the same county. On the two occasions that she saw the spirit she was still in her teens. The house was perhaps only five years old when she first saw the ghost, so the location was not of any real antiquity. Within living memory the site of the house was only open countryside, and no known building formerly occupied the same spot. Perhaps much earlier in history, however, a croft or other building stood there.

Carol was in the hall of the house when she saw the ghost come from the living-room, cross the hall and enter her own bedroom. The spirit was female in form, wearing a long, deep-blue dress that reminded her of the fashion of the Victorian period. The spirit faced Carol for a short time, long enough for her to see her face, and, apart from the fact that the ghost entered her bedroom, Carol was not greatly disturbed by the sighting.

The second time Carol saw the ghost it appeared in the living room. As Carol sat and watched television she became aware of a

158

figure standing by the window. When she turned round to look she saw the same female figure, dressed in the same deep blue clothing. On that occasion the ghost did not move, slowly fading away as she watched it. Carol has had no other experience of seeing ghosts and is not particularly susceptible to sensing any strange presences.

The oldest surviving house in Glasgow is known as Provand's Lordship. It was erected in 1471 as a manse and has had a long and colourful history. Some say that Mary Queen of Scots spent a night there, but more probable was the fact that the house was later home to priests and a hangman. It is the latter's victims that are supposed to haunt the building to this day. The hangman occupied the house in the nineteenth century and he was responsible for carrying out many of the city's executions at that time. He may have been either John Murdoch (who died in 1856 aged about eighty-eight — he was still hanging people in 1851 when it is recorded that he climbed up on to the scaffold with the aid of a stick) or his predecessor, Thomas Young (who died in 1837). Young is known to have executed fifty-six culprits in Glasgow from his appointment in 1814 until his last execution, which was of Hugh Kennedy in

1834. Provand's Lordship stands in Glasgow's High Street, near to the Cathedral. Today the house is protected as a museum by the city council. Tales of haunting have been reported from most of the rooms in the ancient building.

A family living at Buchanan Court in Kirkcaldy seemed to be haunted by a phantom monk. The house stands near Abbotshall, where a monastery existed at one time. During the night the wife awoke to discover the ghostly monk crawling up the bed and trying to choke her. This occurred a number of times, and she could not forget the feeling of the deathly cold hands grasping at her neck. Other members of the family saw the monk on occasions, but only the woman of the house was affected in this way. One night the husband awoke when he heard his wife choking. He turned round to look at her and was terrified to see her face being pressed into the pillow. Some dark figure was on her back carrying out the act. Although the man was able to see that the figure wore a long habit-like cloak, he was unable to make out its face — it was as though there was nothing there. When he let out a loud scream the ghost disappeared. Since that time it has not manifested in the house again, and the wife has been able to sleep soundly at night.

An old building in Linlithgow, West Lothian, is home to a strange spirit that has caused the owners to feel uncomfortable over the years. They feel that Ebenezer Cottage is haunted by something, but have never seen anything. Nevertheless, there is one particular spot in the cottage where the eerie feeling is most noticeable. What causes this strange effect is not known, but it is thought that it may be something to do with the fact that an undertaker at one time used the cottage.

The locals once knew an old house in the High Street of the Kincardineshire town of Stonehaven as the 'Green Lady's House', but it has long since been demolished. Tales of its haunting have been passed down through the families of the residents, and stories linked it with an old tunnel that was supposed to exist from the house to Fetteresso and Dunnottar castles. In 1935, when the cellars of the house were being cleared out, workmen discovered that a secret tunnel did in fact exist, but that it was much shorter than the supposed one to the castles. This one merely connected the house with the shore, and no doubt was created at a time when smuggling was rife on the coastline.

The 'Green Lady's House' was home to an apparition of a woman dressed in a long shiny green dress. It was said that after each

161

appearance, the walls of the house would be covered in a green slime. After the house was demolished the spirit began to appear in other places in the district. She has been witnessed by a number of folk in the area, and there are some who claim that the spirit of a lady seen walking on the Slug Road to the north of the town is the same ghost. In 1956 a lorry driver making his way up the winding road spotted her in the distance. However, as he approached where she should have been, the figure mysteriously disappeared.

A house in Inverness that had formerly been occupied by the guard on the railway is haunted. Today the house operates as a bed and breakfast establishment, and one or two guests have reported seeing spectres within it on various occasions. When Helen MacLellan stayed there she awoke in the middle of the night to witness a man at the foot of her bed. Although rather startled, she watched for a short time and came to the conclusion that he seemed to be washing his face. When she put the light on he disappeared. At other times the sound of footsteps has been heard in the house coming from rooms that are known to be empty.

An old house in Fraserburgh, Aberdeenshire, is said to be home to the manifestation of a Jacobite laird known as 'Old Glenbuchat'. The house, which stands near to the harbour in New Harbour Road, is known to the locals as 'Warld's End', as it formerly stood at the edge of the town, and was the end of the world as far as the townsfolk were concerned. At the beginning of the eighteenth century the house was owned by Lord Glenbuchat, who supported the Jacobite cause. It is claimed that a number of meetings took place here to plot some of the Jacobite rising. Boys living in the town always claimed that Old Glenbuchat still haunted the building, trying to plot the downfall of the Hanoverian royal house.

At Ardgay in Ross-shire an old house suddenly became subjected to a disturbing series of hauntings. The occupier of the house began to hear footsteps in rooms that he knew were empty, and which was confirmed by investigation. He also witnessed one or two items being thrown around a bedroom. At this point he was so scared that he decided to call in the services of a local minister. The man of the cloth went to the house and decided that he would spend the night in the haunted bedroom. It is said that he witnessed the apparition of a woman dressed in black. The spirit was busily occupied near the bed before she disappeared. The minister then carried out an exorcism of the house, and since then the spirit has not returned. Later investigation discovered that the ghostly figure represented a servant girl who had once worked in the house. She had unexpectedly become pregnant, but had kept this secret from everyone. On the birth of the child she suffocated it with a pillow. The corpse was hidden in a drawer for a short period before she was able to smuggle it from the house and bury it in the nearby woods.

A suicide was responsible for the haunting of a house at Ardnadam in Dunoon, Argyll. The owners of the house were frightened one day when they spotted the figure of an old man, dressed in a white top and trousers. It was very distinctive that he wore a red turban on his head, yet his features were decidedly Scottish. On another occasion the occupants of the house heard sounds coming from the attic, as though large boxes were being dragged across the rafters. Research into the history of the house revealed that an old soldier, who had served for many years in India, had formerly owned it. It was during this period that he discovered the turban was an ideal form of headgear for the weather in that subcontinent. In his old age, back in Scotland, he began to suffer from a terminal disease. Realizing this, he went up to the attic of his house where he dragged some large pieces of furniture across the floor in order to bar the door. He then pulled out his gun and shot himself.

A virtually identical tale is related about a house in Edinburgh's Meadow Place. Any witnesses who see this spectre usually do so on the stairs. As they go up or down them the ghost usually passes in the opposite direction. A few sightings of the spirit have also been made in the street outside, and weird bumping sounds have been reported from the attic. It is said that the spirit belongs to a Major Weir, who lived in the house in the late nineteenth century. He was a major in the army, having worked his way up through the ranks. Whilst abroad he made himself a reasonable fortune and was able to purchase this sizeable house back in Edinburgh. The major was also keen on Indian culture, and his neighbours often related that he could, and often did, swear in Hindustani. Major Weir employed an Indian servant and he himself often liked to wear a turban. One day, seemingly out of the blue, the major climbed into the attic of his house and shot himself through the head using his old army gun. It was from that time that the haunting began.

★ ★ ★

Many of Scotland's farmhouses have tales of ghosts associated with them. A great number of these stories are generally unknown, and only through continuous research and listening to traditional tales do many of the following accounts appear in print for the first time. No doubt there are hundreds, if not thousands, of other haunted farms the length and breadth of the country, the tales associated with which are known only to their occupants.

The spirit of a woman haunted an old farmhouse at Glenmallan, which lies three miles north of Garelochhead, Argyll. An old account of the haunting was reported in 1875, by a girl who was staying as a guest at the house. When she entered the bedroom in which she was to sleep, she was surprised to discover that it was already occupied. On the bed, lying on her side and facing into the wall, was a sobbing woman. As the girl approached to find out what was wrong, the ghost disappeared. It was later explained that the spirit probably belonged to the wife of the crofter. She was regularly beaten and abused by her husband, who was a renowned drunkard. Finally, his actions were so severe that his wife died of the injuries sustained. No record of any other sighting has been made since that time.

A farmhouse at Glenbuck in Ayrshire is haunted by a number of young girls. The house at Glenbuck Home Farm was being extended, and to save erecting a new building it was decided to incorporate part of the attic of an adjoining building. Accordingly a doorway was cut through into the new room, which was used as a bedroom. A daughter of the Graham family occupied the room, and on one occasion she awoke to discover three young girls lying on the floor. Within a short time they faded away, and no satisfactory explanation for their presence has ever been given. On another occasion the occupant witnessed one of the girls walking up the stairs of the house. Eventually she decided to tell her mother, and it turned out that she had also seen a young girl on occasion, but had never mentioned it to anyone. It was also thought to be quite significant that whilst the alterations were taking place, a large quantity of arsenic was discovered — too large a quantity to have been kept for agricultural purposes. Who had hidden it in the building and why has never been discovered.

Melville Grange farm stands in a stretch of open countryside that separates Edinburgh and Dalkeith, and was part of Melville Castle estate. The house is said to occupy the site of a much older farmhouse that was at one time part of the estate belonging to the monks of Newbattle Abbey. One of the fourteenth-century monks fell in love with a young woman whose father was a local landowner. They met secretly on many occasions at Melville Grange, but the girl's father discovered who her admirer was. He insisted that she should never meet him again, persuading her that to do so would result in grief for them both. Reluctantly she agreed. However, the girl felt that she would need to explain her position to her friend and so set out to meet her monk and break off the romance.

Her father became aware of the meeting, and thought that his daughter was disobeying him. He followed her to the trysting-place and saw her embrace the monk. Not realizing that his daughter was about to break off the romance, he flew into such a rage that he set the building alight. The flames were quick to take hold, and within a short time the whole farmhouse was ablaze. Both the monk and the girl were killed in the inferno.

Melville Grange farm was rebuilt, but the spirit of the girl has remained. A number of folk over the centuries have claimed to see her, and most describe her as wearing a long white dress. There seem to be no reports of the monk having manifested here.

An old farmhouse or small country house located between Kilsyth and Kirkintilloch was known locally as 'The Haunted House'. Auchinreoch, as it was known, was owned by the Buchanan family, but was abandoned in the early 1800s when they built the more refined Woodburn House. The tenant of Mains of Auchinreoch farm used the old building for a time, but eventually the roof collapsed. What spirit haunts this building is unknown, but it was well known for giving anyone that visited it an uncomfortable feeling.

Further west, at Clachan of Campsie, is Clashmore, scene of a duel in the seventeenth century. Hugh MacFarlane had arranged to meet a son of the Stirling of Glorat family at a spot distinguished by its old chestnut trees. The reason for the duel is not known, but the two families supported opposite sides in those troublesome times — the Stirlings being Royalists and the MacFarlanes, Whigs — and this, no doubt, was the reason for the dispute. The duel took place and MacFarlane won, but he took fright when he realized that his opponent was dead. He hastily dug a shallow grave beneath the trees and buried the corpse there. Many years later a rusty rapier and short dirk were dug up near this spot, and it is assumed that these were Stirling's weapons.

MacFarlane then left the country, joining Marlborough's army and serving as a subaltern. However, being supporters of the Whig government resulted in his family being notified that no proceedings would be taken against him. Since that time the locals claim that the spirit of the Stirling lad has haunted the glen at Clashmore. The ghost appears in the moonlight, wandering from tree to tree.

An old farmhouse situated in Strathtay, a couple of miles north-east of Aberfeldy, Perthshire, is home to the spirit of a young girl. She was a spurned lover, having desires for the son of the farmer there. However, he had no interest in her, and indeed married another. The girl was so distressed by this that she went to the farm and drowned herself in the well. Shortly after the newly-married couple arrived back at the farm they were shocked when the spirit of the girl, her clothes dripping wet, manifested in their bedroom. She was wailing in sadness, and left no trace of water on the floor after she had faded away. Since that first haunting a number of witnesses have heard the watery sound or else caught sight of the girl.

A former mill building at Mansfield Mains farm at New Cumnock in Ayrshire is haunted by a strange presence. The mill is no longer used, having been superseded by modern methods, but the building still stands in a shady grove by the side of its stream. Tales of its haunting abound in the vicinity, though few real sightings have been made. Christopher Donaldson, who stored materials in the building whilst erecting his own house nearby, related that each time he had to go into the old mill to collect or deposit materials, the hairs on his neck would instantly rise. It was as though his sixth sense could detect something that he was unaware of.

A considerable house in the parish of Gairloch in Ross and Cromarty was in the late eighteenth century home to a female ghost. This spectre appeared on various occasions to two different men, 'of the utmost credibility and respectability' according to John Dixon, author of *Gairloch*. She usually manifested in daylight, and the men witnessed her sitting in the building or else walking through its rooms. She was dressed in brown clothing, and on each day she was sighted she mysteriously disappeared and no trace of her could be found. The men attributed her appearance to some incident that was about to take place in the building, but whether anything significant ever did is not known.

To the south of the Borders village of Earlston is Blaikie's Cottage, a typical whitewashed and slated building standing near Craigsford. In the garden is an ancient gravestone commemorating James and Marion Blaikie, as well as their daughter who died in infancy. James himself erected the memorial stone, and it is known that he used to say prayers at it every morning and night for twenty-five years until he died. This happened on 23 June 1749, by which time he was seventy-three years old. But it is not the occupant of this grave that haunts the cottage. A regular visitor to the cottage in more recent years was a woman named Maggie May, who often came to buy fruit that grew in the garden there. After she died, her ghost seems to have decided to make Blaikie's Cottage her home. She wanders around during the night, often seeming to bump into things and make a bit of noise. Nevertheless, Maggie is said to enjoy tidying up after the occupants of the cottage. Often, when the residents of the cottage have gone to bed, Maggie moves things from where they were left lying to where they should be kept.

Near Inverkip in Renfrewshire is an old ruin known to the locals as the Auld Castle. It is properly known as the House of Christwell (Chrisswell on modern maps) and has a long tradition of being haunted. Revd Alexander Peden (c. 1626-1686), known as the 'Prophet of the Covenant', arrived at the door and asked for food and shelter. The occupants of the house, Menteith by name, were opponents of the Covenant and refused him entry. Peden then placed a curse on their home, claiming that it would one day be roofless, its walls would collapse to dust and the public road would, sometime in the future, 'run through the kitchen din'. That was, in fact, exactly what happened. For many years the road from Inverkip to Gourock passed through the middle of the ruins, but these have long since been cleared away.

The knoll that rises to the back of the house has connections with witches, and claims of their appearance have been made on more than one occasion. One particular tale relates that a young drummer in the army returned home from the war one winter's evening. As he passed the haunted house he was pursued by one of the witches, disguised as a werewolf. She bit into his flesh and then destroyed his body so completely that locals found bits of it spread over a large area the following morning.

Another ghost associated with the House of Christwell manifested as a pirate. He was said to wander through the Spango valley and surrounding moors brandishing his cutlass. Some accounts claim that he carried a skull and crossbones flag and that he was sometimes seen counting his pieces of eight. There have also been reports of a pair of spirits wandering in the vicinity of the house in the middle of the night. Dressed in pristine white grave-clothes, this pair is reckoned to be a newly-married couple who lived at Christwell, but who died rather suddenly for some unknown reason.

The death of a young lad resulted in the haunting of an old house in the village of Avoch, which lies on the Black Isle, north of Inverness. The boy was in his bed sleeping when he suddenly pulled back the covers. Stepping from his bed he sleepwalked across the room towards the window. Sliding up the sash he leaned too far out of it and fell to his death on the ground below. Since that time the bedroom has been home to various strange happenings, from weird noises heard in the night, to objects being moved around when no one was present in the house. The type of object most commonly moved was toys, which points towards the spirit being that of the young lad who tragically died. On the odd occasion the faint apparition of the young lad has been seen, but he does not appear to manifest very often.

At Tain in Ross-shire, the spirit of a man walking a dog haunted an old house. He would appear in one corner of a bedroom and walk through objects and walls. The Richardson family occupied the house in Tower Street and it was their two-year-old daughter, Nicole, who witnessed the strange phenomena on a number of occasions. She hated her bedroom, and did not want to return to what she described as the 'bad house' when she was away visiting friends or relatives. On one occasion the girl claimed that the ghostly figure tried to enter her bed.

The haunting continued for some time, with Nicole waking up in the middle of the night, screaming, 'Man, man, man'. As time went on she was disturbed more regularly. The parents took the girl to their general practitioner, who told them that she was too young to make up such things. Although Kevin and Jill Richardson had never seen the ghost, they were disturbed by various inexplicable happenings in their home. They heard various noises that could never be explained, and a number of times returned home to find that the lights had mysteriously switched themselves on, when they were definitely switched off on leaving. On other occasions the telephone would suddenly go dead and then come on again, and various parts of the house seemed to be freezing cold.

At length the Richardsons decided to call in the services of Dornoch Cathedral's

Church of Scotland minister. The Revd Susan Brown paid the house a visit in May 1999 and prayed that the spirits should leave the house and let the occupants live in peace. However, the Richardson family had already decided to move out, being unwilling to stay in the property. They were frightened that the ghost might follow them to their new home.

A similar tale of haunting has been reported in a house at Girdle Toll, in Irvine, Ayrshire. Mr and Mrs White and their five children were terrified when they witnessed the spirit of a man storming across the living-room of their home. When he reached the corner he leaned over and berated a young girl, perhaps aged about seven. The man tends to laugh hysterically and for some reason or another wears strange clothing. The family claimed that this man terrified them so much that they were all forced to sleep in the same room. Eventually some of them had to flee the house and seek the safety of relatives' homes. One night Margaret White awoke to see the man at the foot of her bed. When she screamed loudly he disappeared.

The White family says that the spirit even dragged one of them by the feet from their bed. It was only when they were rudely awakened from their sleep that the spectre eventually went away.

The White family had only occupied the house for a short time before the haunting started. However, Alex and Mary Cuthbertson had reported strange happenings at this house over the previous twenty years. The list is lengthy, and includes weird occurrences like objects moving by themselves, a crucifix lighting up, names being called in the middle of the night, and electrical appliances starting by themselves. Mary Cuthbertson claimed that the spectre of the young girl would regularly pull her husband's hair as he sat in his chair in the living-room. She too has seen the girl, and described her as looking rather transparent, rather like an X-ray.

It has been claimed that a previous occupant of the house was a medium and that she was responsible for causing almost two hundred different ghosts to haunt the building. A ghostly girl was said to have squirted perfume at a witness on one occasion, and on others the residents saw faces surrounded by what appeared to be clouds. The tenants have heard the noise of foot-stamping and clapping, and more than once they have been shocked when objects lifted up into the air by themselves.

8

Weird Places

Spectres do not limit their appearances to places of great antiquity, where evil deeds from the past may have taken place; deeds which were sometimes recorded in history, sometimes totally forgotten. Ghosts have appeared in many strange places, from hospitals to offices, theatres to ships. This chapter will look at a number of these hauntings.

Hospitals are quite often haunted according to those who work there. At least three different hospitals in Glasgow are claimed to be haunted. The Royal Infirmary is one of the city's oldest medical establishments, having been incorporated by George III in 1791 and open for treatment two years later. Many alterations have been made to the building over the years, and today it presents a massive bulk on the city landscape, dwarfing the cathedral that stands alongside.

The Royal Infirmary is home to a Green Lady. At some point in the hospital's history, staff were caring for a patient with an excitable nature. Suddenly the patient jumped from his bed and ran along the ward to the doorway. He managed to escape into the corridor and was about to commit suicide when a nurse caught up with him. As she tried to prevent him from jumping over the banister she was caught up in the struggle and was pushed over herself. She fell into the stair-well and a few storeys to the ground floor. Despite attempts at resuscitating her she died shortly after.

Since that time a ghost has haunted the surgical block of the hospital. A number of different medical staff have seen her, and sightings have taken place at all times of the day and night. It has also been reported that the Green Lady has a helpful nature, and when she appears she is usually trying to assist in some way or other.

In the same city, at Gilmorehill, is the Western Infirmary. This hospital dates from 1871 but it has been extended considerably since. Unlike the Royal Infirmary, it is known who the ghost at the Western Infirmary was in life. Sir William MacEwen (1848–1924) was a distinguished neurosurgeon who worked in the buildings. He developed brain surgery considerably, pioneering operations for tumours, abscesses and trauma.

One of the stories told in the infirmary is

that shortly before he died, MacEwen was asked to perform an operation on a young artist. The painter suffered from severe migraine headaches and it was hoped that MacEwen would be able to cure this problem. For some reason or other, MacEwen refused to perform the operation. The artist, angered at the response, and suffering a bout of headache, jumped down four flights of stairs. He was killed instantly.

Since MacEwen's death, numerous people have made sightings of him, including witnesses in recent times who did not know him. Most sightings have him disappearing into thin air outside the operating theatre where he worked. It has been claimed that the spectre of the surgeon haunts the hospital due to the remorse he felt in refusing to operate on the artist.

The Gartloch Hospital is located on the east side of Glasgow, between Garthamlock and Gartcosh, but no longer operates as such. Some of the nurses in the hospital reported seeing an apparition of a woman dressed in black. She usually appeared in the vicinity of Ward 1, and those who witnessed her were able to see her make her way along the corridor. At first they usually thought that this was an old woman who had lost her way in the hospital, but they were soon to realize that it was in fact a ghost when she disappeared through an old doorway that had been boarded up for many years. This had led to speculation that the woman was a matron or nurse from the early days of the hospital.

Ballochmyle Hospital near Mauchline in Ayrshire was originally built as a temporary facility during the Second World War. It was eventually replaced in 2000 by a new hospital in the nearby town of Cumnock. The old hospital was where plastic surgery was developed. Ward 14 was home to a Grey Lady that has manifested a couple of times. Around 1988 Karen Thomson, who worked as a nurse in that ward, was working on the night shift. When it was time for her tea break she spotted an old lady who had long grey hair. At first she wondered who this was, but within a few minutes the apparition had faded away.

A former poorhouse, located near Logierait village in Perthshire, was claimed to be one of the most haunted buildings in Scotland by the woman who owned it in the 1990s. Cuil na Daraich was erected in 1863 as a workhouse, and bore the title, 'The Atholl, Weem and Breadalbane Combination Poor House'. Around 110 men, women and children were housed in its many rooms at a time, but it was later converted into an old folk's home. In 1989 Tina Reynolds bought the building and opened it as a museum of childhood.

During her restoration work she witnessed many strange sightings. Men and women would walk past her as she worked, disappearing just as quickly as they had appeared. She has also seen two young boys, whom she thought were aged around eight or nine, who ran around the building causing mayhem wherever they went. Hundreds of visitors to the museum began reporting that they had witnessed some form of ghost or manifestation within the building. One of these tourists was a psychic and he claimed that he saw spirits of men, women and children in every corner of every room.

Tina's daughter, Sam, stayed in the building for five nights, and she later related to her mother that on every single night when she went to bed, she felt the foot of the bed suddenly sink as though someone had sat down on it. At first she jumped up to see who it was, but discovered that no one was there. On further visits made over the years by Sam, the invisible person who sat there all night no longer bothered her. It is quite eerie to consider that when Tina's aged mother spent a night in the same bed, and not knowing the story, she too experienced the same feeling.

The National Library of Scotland, which is located in Edinburgh, is home to a strange ghost. In an area of the library known as the vaults, the spectre of a highland chieftain has been seen on occasion. One of the sightings took place in 1973 when a member of staff at the library, Elizabeth Clark, was sent down to the vaults to file away some papers and books. The area had a reputation for being haunted, but Elizabeth had no real thoughts on the matter. However, when she turned from her work she spotted a large figure of a man, dressed in the garb of a clan chieftain. Quite distinctive was the intricate silver brooch holding his plaid together, decorated with Celtic knot work. The highlander held out his hands to her, and she noticed that they were manacled together by a stout chain. Elizabeth was shocked at the sight, so she muttered a silent prayer to herself and rushed out of the area. She later discovered that the library occupied the site of a nineteenth-century prison that was often used for imprisoning debtors.

★   ★   ★

There are claims that a number of schools are haunted in some way or other. The author works in one where tales have been told of strange supernatural occurrences. The present Irvine Royal Academy building was erected in 1969 on a site that had once been used for other purposes during the Second World War. Whether or not this has anything to do with the occurrences in the school is not known. Apart from a few early claims of folk having seen a ghost at what is described as the back of the school, one incident that occurred in the late 1990s was quite distinctive.

Duncan Lindsay, who works in the school as the technician, was in his room after the bell had gone to announce the end of the pupils' working day. His room is located between two classrooms, to which it is connected by doors. As he worked in his room he was suddenly aware of the light that streamed in through the keyhole going dark before appearing again, as though someone in the classroom had walked past the door. Thinking that it was a cleaner, he opened the door to speak to them. However, he found the room totally empty. Just as he was wondering what could have caused the stream of light to end for a few seconds, he noticed a book that was perched on a rack fall over by itself. Within seconds the next book along fell in a similar way, and was closely followed by a few others. Frightened out of his wits, Duncan Lindsay returned to his own room and locked the door!

A strange spirit also haunts Bo'ness Academy in West Lothian. This one has been seen, however, and takes the form of a young lady who dresses in rather modern clothing. This spectre usually appears in the morning, just after the cleaners arrive to commence work. In 1996 one of the cleaners, Mary Cunningham, reported that she felt some form of presence behind her. She turned round and saw the youngish female figure, who had fair hair and was dressed in a casual manner. At first she did not realize that the apparition was a ghost, but when it reached out to touch her she screamed, causing it to disappear. As a result of her experience, she was so frightened that she was off work for a couple of days. A workmate, Maisie King, also witnessed the ghost, and like Mary Cunningham reported it to their supervisor, who had also been aware of some form of presence in the building. Who the spirit was is not known, but from its modern dress and youngish appearance, it has been speculated that the ghost is the spirit of a former pupil who may have been killed in an unfortunate accident.

A pupil who was staying at an outdoor residential centre experienced another strange sight. Gordon Sloan, of Auchinleck, Ayrshire, was still a pupil at Ochiltree Primary School when he went on a course at Kames Outdoor Centre at nearby Muirkirk. The centre is located in what was a miners' institute, where meetings of all sorts were held, and where miners could relax by playing billiards and other games. However, this does not help to explain what he saw. During the night Gordon awoke in his dormitory and when he looked at the foot of his bed he saw a ghostly figure of a man on horseback. He was wearing a long cloak that hung down over the horse. It was standing in the middle of the room, and Gordon was quite surprised at what he saw. He reached up to wake the boy sleeping on the bunk above, but when he awoke the covers fell from the upper bunk obscuring his view. When he was able to pull the sheet aside the spectre had disappeared. Although he witnessed the ghost more than twenty years ago, he is convinced that he saw the ghostly rider, and says that he will never forget the sight as long as he lives.

Reid Kerr College is located in Paisley, to the west of Glasgow. Strange occurrences in their pottery rooms troubled the art department staff in the 1980s. Over a period of time various items went missing, and everyone was at a loss to explain where the items went.

Theft seemed to be unlikely due to the type of items missing, but as a precaution the two doors leading into the pottery rooms were locked. The doors were even kept locked when students were using the equipment, but one day those working at the wheels heard the sound of the doors being unlocked. Footsteps were heard making their way down the corridor, but when they went to see who was coming no one could be seen. This happened a few times and in every case the corridor was empty.

On other occasions the pottery room went inexplicably cold and heavy barrels of liquid glaze were found moved to places where they did not belong. These things were hard to explain, for the room was usually quite warm, and the tubs of glaze normally required three men to lift when they were full. The strange happenings in the college seem to have abated in recent years.

In Aberdeen the Robert Gordon University incorporates an old building erected in 1739 as Robert Gordon's Hospital. Merchant venturer, Robert Gordon (1668–1731), earned his fortune in the Baltic trade, and a hospital for the education of scholars was established in accordance with the wishes of his will. It became Robert Gordon's College in 1881 and in 1992 was established as a university.

During the Jacobite uprising the original building was taken over by the Hanoverian soldiers and it is claimed that during this time one of them murdered a servant here. According to tradition her blood left stains on the floor that were impossible to remove. Indeed, they only disappeared when the floor was eventually lifted and new boards laid at the time of restoration. During the night when the building is empty, caretakers and janitors have heard strange noises, and it is claimed that they come from the ghost of the murdered servant.

Office blocks of various vintages have had ghostly sightings within them. The headquarters of Aberdeen City Council, located in St Nicolas House, have a strange spirit within them that seems to be quite unique. Within recent years a number of employees have reported seeing a phantom male. Two separate women, who had neither met nor spoken to each other before the incident, watched as a spectre walked along the corridor and entered a lift. The doors closed for a few seconds before opening again, as one of the women had just pressed the button. The lift did not have sufficient time to go up or down, but when the doors reopened the man had gone.

The headquarters of North Ayrshire Council are located in Cunninghame House, a modern office block in the centre of Irvine. The building was only erected in 1976, but it occupies the site of a fourteenth-century Carmelite friary. This explains the spirit that has been witnessed on a number of occasions. Jim McCarten, a chief council officer who works in the building, first saw the ghost in 1989. He was working on the fourth floor, checking that the building was empty and the locks secure. Suddenly he was aware of something out of the corner of his eye. He turned quickly and saw a figure dressed in a monk's habit. It was only a fleeting glance, but then the apparition disappeared through a wall. Jim's second sighting also took place on the fourth floor. He was walking along the corridor when he heard a very loud clunking sound. He turned round, and his senses told him that the sound was coming from near the fire extinguisher. As he looked he was given another short sighting of the same monk passing by. Jim claims that this time he was left terrified, and the hairs on the back of his neck really stood on end. Other workers, particularly cleaners who are in the building when it is relatively quiet, have also witnessed the spectre.

The former offices of the *Scotsman* newspaper are situated in Edinburgh's North Bridge. The building was purpose-built for the newspaper in 1899–1902, but in 1999 the offices were closed when the newspaper moved to a more modern building. The original building was then converted into a hotel. There is a long-standing belief that the building is haunted. Some folk claim that the ghost they saw was the manifestation of an early printer. Sporting a beard, he would appear in various rooms within the large complex. Others claimed that there was a ghostly forger who worked in the building. Claims have been made that this spirit was responsible for printing good-quality copies of Scottish pound notes in the 1930s. In 1994 one of the employees of the *Evening News*, a *Scotsman* newspaper, witnessed the ghost in the basement of the building. The spectre was making its way along the corridor with an old 'galley', or tray, in which type was set. It was even able to pass through a locked door, and the witness was extremely disturbed by what he saw.

Also in the city is a restaurant known as 'Les Partisans', where the spirits of many children have been sensed, although no one has ever seen them. The restaurant used to be a waxworks museum, but prior to that it operated as a children's home. The ghosts are usually experienced in the main hall of the building, and the sound of their feet shuffling is apparent. The children also seem to whisper to each other across the hall.

* * *

Prisons have ghostly spirits within them too. The tolbooth in Stirling is an old building that was erected in 1703 to act as a burgh court and gaol. The building still stands, but it is many years since prisoners were held there. In 1999 work commenced on restoring the building in order to create a centre for arts, crafts and drama. Tales of the haunting of the tolbooth are of long standing in the town. This goes back to 1843 when 84-year-old Allan Mair was hanged at the town's market cross for killing his wife. His death was so gruesome that he became the last man to have a public execution in Stirling. His body was then removed and tradition claims that he was buried in the floor of the tolbooth. Since then his ghostly spirit has disturbed tenants of the building.

During the renovation work on the building, archaeologists were called in to excavate its foundations. In May 2000 a rough wooden coffin was found beneath the concrete floor of a corridor, and when it was opened a body was discovered within. It was quite unique in that the very shoes he wore

191

on the day of his execution still survived, wrapped around the skeletal foot.

The gaol at Jedburgh in the Borders was erected in 1820–3 to the plans of Archibald Elliot. A rather fine castellated building, it was one of the earliest modern prisons, built to replace the old tolbooths. Following John Howard's 'Reformatory Imprisonment' principles, the gaol offered inmates a comparatively comfortable cell, with a chance to exercise in the enclosed yards. The prison occupies the site of the ancient castle of Jedburgh, which was demolished by the Scots in 1409 to prevent it falling into English hands once more.

The ghost in the gaol has its origins back in the year 1285. In October that year, King Alexander III married for a second time in the great hall of the castle. His bride was Yolande of Druix, a young and beautiful woman. At the wedding feast he became aware of a strange spirit in the building. Most of the guests were aware of it also. It seemed to come straight towards him, making its way through the dancing guests. Dressed in ragged grave-clothes, the figure's face was covered by a mask, down which rivulets of blood poured. The spectre spoke slowly. 'Alexander will die soon enough,' it warned.

The king did not know what to think, but

ordered his men to seize the intruder and put him to death at sunrise. The soldiers advanced towards the figure, but soon were transfixed in terror. They were unable to arrest the figure and it managed to escape.

A Border seer, Thomas the Rhymer, who was well known for his accurate gift of prophecy, was to tell the Earl of March that the sixteenth day of March would be one of the stormiest days that Scotland would ever experience. When that day arrived those who knew the prophecy were surprised to discover that it was a calm and pleasant winter morning. On that day King Alexander was riding along the coast of Fife, heading home to his bride. Suddenly, at Kinghorn, his horse reared up and threw him off its back. He fell down a cliff and was killed. A memorial marks the spot where he died. The storm that the Rhymer referred to was said to be the troubles that then commenced amongst the claimants to the throne, including the English presence, and subsequent battle for independence.

The ghost at Jedburgh has been witnessed on other occasions. Every time he is seen, some form of death seems to take place shortly afterwards. This harbinger of death has not made any known appearances in recent years. The tale, however, is thought to have given Edgar Allan Poe the inspiration for his tale *The Masque of the Red Death*.

★ ★ ★

Most of Scotland's theatres have tales of ghosts that haunt them. In Edinburgh the Festival Theatre is home to a spirit that is claimed to be the Great Lafayette. Sigmund Neuberger (1873–1911) was a magician and illusionist who appeared on stage with the name the Great Lafayette. He appeared all over the world, and in 1911 he was starring at the Empire Palace Theatre in Edinburgh. He thrilled the audience with his amazing display of tricks, which included his apparent ability to transfer himself from one place to another. During one of his main sketches, which involved a live lion, the theatre caught fire, and within a short time the flames had engulfed the stage. A spark landed on the lion, setting his mane alight, and within seconds it was running around the stage roaring in pain. The Great Lafayette tried to follow the creature in order to shoot it, therefore putting it out of its misery. However, he died in the smoke along with nine others.

After the flames were doused the investigators discovered that an electrical fault had been responsible for the disaster. Searching the wreckage, they found the body of a man wearing Lafayette's sword. He was taken to Glasgow for cremation, but further investigation unearthed a second body that was proved to belong to the illusionist. It turned out that he used a double in his act — a fact that few people were aware of.

The theatre was reopened following some restoration work, but within time degenerated into a bingo hall. In 1994 the building was rebuilt and opened as the Edinburgh Festival Theatre. Since that time the manifestation of a tall dark figure has been seen many times, and it is claimed that it is the spirit of the Great Lafayette. Witnesses include a cleaner and a stagehand employed in the theatre. Most of the sightings seem to take place at the spot where Lafayette's real body was found, even though the theatre has been rebuilt with a different layout.

The city's Playhouse Theatre stands in Greenside Place, at the head of Leith Walk, at the east end of the New Town. The theatre was opened in 1929 as a dual-purpose cinema and theatre, with seating for over three thousand people. Many of those who trod the boards in the theatre have witnessed the resident ghost, named Albert. It has been claimed that he is the spirit of an old stagehand who died in an accident early in the life of the theatre. Others claim that he was a night watchman who committed suicide. The scariest spot in the theatre seems to be on level six, where it can suddenly turn cold for no apparent reason.

It is said that Albert is a friendly, but mischievous spectre, responsible for inexplicable happenings. These vary from switching lights on and off to moving things from one place to another. On one occasion the burglar alarm went off at the theatre one morning. The police were called and sniffer dogs searched the building. Although the dogs were rather restless in the theatre, the police reported that they could find no break-in, and all that they saw was an old man in a grey coat. When told that there should have been no one at all in the building, they realized that they had probably witnessed the spirit of Albert.

The Royal Lyceum Theatre in Grindlay Street is home to a female ghost who seems to manifest on a high balcony. It is mainly actors looking up to the balcony that witness her. Nobody should be in this area during performances as the area is now filled with lights and wiring, even though there are still seats. Those who have seen her describe the spirit as wearing a long blue dress. Some think that it may be the manifestation of Dame Ellen Terry (1848–1928). She was a popular actress and performed at the official opening of the Royal Lyceum in 1883. For many years a statue of her graced the foyer.

The Citizens' Theatre in Glasgow is located in Gorbals Street on the south side of the Clyde. The spirit of a Green Lady has been reported on a number of occasions. The Citizens' Theatre was built in 1878 as Her Majesty's Theatre, later renamed the Royal Princess Theatre, and given its present name in 1945. Sometime in its early life it is said that a front-of-house manageress committed suicide by jumping from the upper circle. Since that time the spectre of the manageress has manifested in a pale green form, flitting around in dark corners. Naturally, most of the sightings have taken place in the upper circle, but she has been seen elsewhere in the building.

A lady of a different hue haunts Perth Theatre, which stands in the town's High Street. In 1924, when the theatre was partially destroyed in a fire, the first sightings of the Grey Lady were made, and since that time various actors and stagehands have witnessed her. Like all theatre ghosts, she tends to manifest in dark areas of the building. Perth Theatre has also witnessed a number of other inexplicable happenings. On odd occasions the tip-up seats have been known to drop down loudly by themselves, only to jump back up later.

The Byre Theatre in St Andrews was established in 1933 when a disused byre was converted for theatrical purposes. In 1970 this building was demolished and a new purpose-built theatre was erected on the same spot in the town's Abbey Street. The quaint name connecting it with the old byre was kept.

In the old theatre building, people were most likely to feel the spectre when walking up a set of stairs heading towards the Green Room. The sensation they experienced was the feeling that someone or something had squeezed its way past, and then pushed them to one side. Of course, no one could be seen. When this happened the temperature in the stairwell would usually drop considerably. Workers at the theatre christened the ghost 'Charlie', but he has not been felt since the theatre was rebuilt. The name was chosen in honour of Charles Manford, who kept the theatre open throughout the war years, virtually running it single-handedly. He later became director at the 'Old Vic' in London and died in 1955. Whether or not the spirit belongs to him or someone else is another matter.

The Rialto cinema in Dundee occupied a building that was formerly a theatre; it was converted when celluloid became more popular than live acts. In the 1950s a projectionist was working in the projection room with his back to the door. As he spliced a broken film he heard the door open behind him, and someone enter the room before closing the door behind them. The man thought that it was a workmate, and he told him that he wouldn't be long. He did not turn round as he was concentrating on the task in front of him at the time. However, when he had completed the mend, he turned round and was astonished to discover that he was still in the room by himself.

Whereas most of the theatres mentioned have spectres associated with people who worked in them, the ghost that haunts Eden Court Theatre in Inverness is different. The theatre was erected in 1976 on the site of an old bishop's palace, fragments of which are incorporated into the modern building. The Green Room in the theatre was formed out of the old chapel. The manifestation that appears there is said to be the ghost of one of the bishop's wives. According to tradition she committed suicide by hanging herself within the palace. Since that time a Green Lady has haunted the site, and since the theatre was built she has made the building her home. One of the most common forms of evidence for her is the sound of footsteps making their way across rooms and down corridors. When these areas are checked to see if someone has entered them without permission, no one can ever be found.

A major tragedy took place at the Glen cinema in Paisley on Hogmanay 1929. During a children's matinée performance, the reel of film overheated and caught fire. The operator managed to douse the flames but the smoke frightened the children and panic broke out in the auditorium. The children all tried to leave at once, trampling over each other in a mad dash for the fire exit. The stampede caused many to collapse and they were either killed from the crush or else from the asphyxiation that followed. In total sixty-nine youngsters died, and a memorial commemorates them in Paisley's Hawkhead cemetery.

The site of the Glen cinema is now occupied by a furniture store and the staff have discovered that the building seems to be haunted by the spirits of the dead children. In the basement of the shop staff are convinced that the children are playing jokes on them by moving items around or switching lights on and off. When the shop manager was descending the steps to the basement one day he was convinced that someone was following him. He could hear the footsteps on the stairs behind him, but when he turned round to see who it was there was no one there. On another occasion the members of staff were heading home when they suddenly realized that they had left the lights on in the shop. A special trip was made back to the building in Paisley's town centre to switch them off. However, when they returned to the shop on Monday they found that the lights had mysteriously switched themselves back on again.

A supermarket in Elgin is home to a spectre that comes out at night. Workers in Safeway who have been in the building after dark, when the shop is closed to the public, have experienced the strange sight of a dark man wearing a hooded cloak. He has been blamed for various strange happenings that have taken place in the shop. One night a member of staff was walking down one of the aisles when she noticed a stand containing leaflets was shaking slightly. Suddenly the brochures flew up into the air and landed all over the floor. She went to the spot to see what had caused this, but found nothing. As she tidied up the mess she heard a masculine giggle. No one was in the vicinity, however.

Other members of staff in the supermarket have seen the caped ghost at various times throughout the night. Some have heard it mutter things to them, but have not been able to make out what it was saying. From the hooded description it has been speculated that the spirit may belong to a monk of the Grey Friars order — a monastery that was burned at the reformation previously occupied the site where the supermarket now stands.

★ ★ ★

Factories can also be haunted. The Ravenscraig steelworks were at one time the largest such works in Scotland. In the past decade the factory has been closed and today there is little to indicate that at one time thousands of people worked among the huge blast furnaces and steel-rolling mills. In the late 1960s some of the workers at the factory began to see the manifestation of a steelworker. The figure was dressed not unlike them, but seemed to be wearing clothing from a slightly earlier period in the factory's history. Most of the sightings occurred near to blast furnace no. 2 and, apart from the strange clothing, most workers were unaware that the figure was a ghost until he disappeared. More ready to admit that the man was indeed a spectre were those who, when he appeared before them, saw him as a headless figure.

Still intact, but now preserved as an industrial museum, is the Verdant Jute Works in Dundee. This building was erected in 1833 as the High Mill of the Verdant Works. It employed five hundred people at the height of production, but trade dwindled over the years and it closed at the turn of the century. Since that time it has had various uses, but in 1991 Dundee Heritage Trust acquired the building and began the process of restoring it, and it is now open to the public.

In 1852 a young female worker got caught up in a drive-belt that operated one of the machines. A shaft suspended from the ceiling drove the belt, and the girl was hauled up into the roof space of the mill. She fell from there to the floor and was killed. In the following year a similar accident claimed the life of a man at the works. Speculation claims that it was one of these two deaths that resulted in the present haunting of the building. No one has seen the spectre, so cannot comment on whether it takes a male or female form. However, after the museum is closed for the night it has been reported that lights and machinery are able to switch themselves on and off. Sometimes the rooms can suddenly turn icy cold. The caretaker reported that he thought one of the doors or windows must be open, but a search revealed that all were closed, and no reason for the chill could be found.

Other strange events that have occurred at the factory include things moving by themselves from one place to another, and the sound of doors banging shut minutes after they were closed. On a number of occasions the police have called out the caretaker because they were convinced the building had been broken into. The alarm had gone off and the police could hear loud noises coming from within. When the caretaker carried out a search of the building nothing untoward was discovered, and no sign of forced entry was found.

In the same city is a haunted ship. RRS *Discovery* was built in 1899 and launched from Dundee Shipbuilding Company's yard. After serving as Captain Robert Scott's research ship, taking him to the Antarctic, it was preserved in London before being brought to Dundee in 1986 where it is the central attraction at Discovery Point in the docklands area of the city. Today the ship is open as a museum and interpretation centre. Some folk claim that the spirit of Charles

Bonner, one of the crew members, haunts the ship. In 1901 he was carrying out his duty in the crow's nest when he accidentally fell on to the deck below. He was found dead by other members of the crew and his spirit was said to have haunted the ship thereafter. He is blamed for footsteps that are heard on the deck above, when it is known that no one on board is responsible for them. The officers' wardroom on the ship is located directly below the deck where Bonner would have landed, and many visitors have felt rather uneasy when they approach it. Indeed, many of the visitors touring the ship have refused to enter this room.

Other accounts of the haunting of the *Discovery* claim that the ghost belongs to Ernest Shackleton, an Irish explorer who died on board the ship during an Antarctic expedition in 1922. Robert Conway worked as a guide on the ship and regularly experienced the strange footsteps. He also reported that one particular bulb, located over Shackleton's bunk, would blow on a regular basis. Although electricians checked the wiring thoroughly to try and find out what was wrong, nothing was discovered to explain this anomaly. On one occasion a visitor entered the room and said hello to someone. Conway asked her who she was talking to, as there was no one else there. She replied, 'The man in the corner'. The woman was able to give a detailed description of the man she had seen, and from this it was deduced that it was probably Ernest Shackleton.

In Rutherglen, which lies to the south-east of Glasgow, is a snooker club that has a reputation for being haunted. Two separate owners of the hall have witnessed paranormal activity within the building. Amongst the strange things that have been seen are snooker balls that apparently move by themselves. On one occasion a psychic fair was held in the hall, and it has been claimed that the ghost that frequented the building was laid to rest at that time.

One of the most remote haunted buildings in Scotland must be Eilean Mor Lighthouse, which is located on the largest of the Flannan Isles, which lie to the west of Lewis. The lighthouse was erected in 1899 in order to guide ships around the west coast of Scotland, where the rocks and tides created a treacherous stretch of water for sailors to navigate. In the last few weeks of 1900 the three lighthouse keepers on duty were Thomas Marshall (Head Keeper), James Ducat and Donald MacArthur. On 15 December the light on the rock mysteriously went out, despite many built-in safeguards. Shipping suddenly became aware of the danger, and sent signals back ashore to warn others. Due to weather conditions it was not until Boxing Day that a party was able to land on the rock and begin an investigation. When they tied up at the quay they were surprised to discover that no one came out to greet them.

A search of the tiny islet and its lighthouse was made. None of the keepers was found, and there was nothing to indicate where they had disappeared to. The dining-table still had a meal of cold meat, pickles and potatoes on it, and one kitchen chair was knocked over. The only thing that could not be accounted for was a rather strange piece of seaweed that was unrecognizable to the rescue crew, despite their long years at sea. The lighthouse logbook was inspected to see if it could shed any light on the mystery. Some of this read:

December 12: Gale north by north-west. Sea lashed to fury. Never seen such a storm. Waves very high, tearing at lighthouse. Everything shipshape. James Ducat irritable.
[later] Storm still raging, wind steady. Stormbound. Cannot go out. Ship passing sounding foghorn. Could see lights of

cabins. Ducat quiet. Donald MacArthur crying.

December 13: Storm continued through night. Wind shifted west by north. Ducat quiet. MacArthur praying.

[later] Noon. Grey daylight. Me, Ducat and MacArthur prayed.

December 14: [logbook blank]

December 15: Storm ended, sea calm. God is over all.

Why the men had been so terrified cannot be explained. The storm was not exceptional by Atlantic standards; indeed, twenty miles away on the island of Lewis there was no evidence of it. What made them turn to prayer the way they did is not known, and the mysterious last entry, 'God is over all', left the mystery of their disappearance even deeper.

During an inquiry that took place into the missing keepers, it was questioned why the men would sit out the storm but insist on leaving the island by boat once the storm had settled. This was something that a lighthouse keeper's honour would not allow him to do, and that three did it at once was unusual. A ship that passed the lighthouse on 15 December had noticed that there was no light. Within a short time they spotted a boat with three men on board, rowing through the darkness. As they passed by the ship's bow, they called out to the men, asking if they wished to come aboard. No reply was forthcoming, and the men disappeared into the night. They were never seen again and it is thought that the sight of the boat was a ghostly vision of the keepers who died.

One of the other theories to explain the missing lighthouse-keepers claimed that the ghost of St Flannan arrived on the islet and claimed their souls.

⋆ ⋆ ⋆

There are various accounts of ghosts that have manifested underground. At New Cumnock in Ayrshire there was a former coal mine known as Knockshinnoch Castle Colliery. The pit was sunk between the wars. On 7 September 1950 there was a major disaster when the ceiling of the rising shaft collapsed, allowing the peat moss overhead to fill the mine. Thirteen men were killed and a further 116 trapped. They remained underground for some time until a rescue attempt managed to free them. The whole story was made into a film, *The Brave Don't Cry*.

The colliery had a reputation for being haunted by the spectre of a miner. A pit electrician, John MacKnight, was working below ground one day. He was repairing electrical panels when he became aware of someone standing beside him. Although he knew that he should have been in that part of the mine by himself, he remained unperturbed. As he worked the figure gave him advice, telling him that he had made a mistake. Looking at his work he realized his error and corrected it before finishing the job. It was then he noticed that the person had disappeared. Back on the surface he inquired as to who was down with him, but no one could think who it might be. The man in charge of checking everyone in and out was convinced that no one had joined him. That was when they realized that some form of spectre had been witnessed.

The ghost in Knockshinnoch Castle pit may perhaps be a modern version of the original Knockshinnoch ghost. The pit was named after an old tower house that stood at Knockshinnoch farm nearby. The building has long been demolished, but stories of its spectre were often related in the district. Helen J. Steven wrote of the ghost in 1899:

An old man, who is still alive, tells a tale of going to the lonely tower with a companion. Forgetful of ghostly visitors, and not thinking of any danger in the daytime, they

210

entered the ancient building. Hardly had they crossed the threshold when a feeling of oppression overcame them; terrific bursts of noise broke forth about them and shook the very walls. Terror-stricken they fled to the dwelling-house of Knockshinnoch, where the story told to the farmer and his wife was received in sympathetic silence, for the mysterious sounds were well known to the good folks themselves. Together they returned and gazed once more upon the tower, but no sound greeted their ears, and no rents were visible in the ancient walls. The sun shone brightly on the peaceful scene, and the whole tale seemed unreal and fanciful, and yet they all knew it true. At the same farm at one time there was a servant called Turley. Turley was the most practical man in the world, but even he fell a victim to the little blindfold god who sends his shafts so much at random. Turley's sweetheart was a servant lass, and the course of true love had apparently no great obstacles to surmount. And yet Turley had a drop of gall in the sweetness of his cup — his fellow ploughmen teased him unmercifully, and in the gloamin' hour, when Turley was wont to walk with his lady fair, their remarks were not conducive to that repose of mind for which poor Turley sighed. The tower had an uncanny reputation, but Turley's imagination had not been cultivated and his mind was not active enough for such tales as were often told in his hearing, to move him at all. The sweetheart was a matter-of-fact young person with no undue nonsense about her, and Turley and she agreed to make the tower their trysting-place. There they were safe from prying eyes and scathing remarks, and there in the gloamin' they met time and again. One evening they sat together in a small recess in the wall of the tower, when suddenly over the languorous heat of the summer eve fell a chill, intense as the snows of winter or the touch of a dying hand. Turley and his sweetheart shuddered in affright and gazed on each other enquiringly. In another moment they heard a faint sound of rustling, and a lady of stately mien glided across the room. Her face, full in their vision, was pale and expressionless, her dress rustled as she walked, but there was no sound of footfall. She disappeared as mysteriously as she had come. Perhaps it was a trick, but the lovers thought otherwise. Turley with his prospective bride never visited the tower again. But that was not all. A young man was passing the tower one day, when, to his amazement, he heard strains of music proceeding from the interior. He listened for a time, and the music seemed to him the most lovely that ever fell on mortal ear. He went to the farmhouse and told the folks of what he had heard. They laughed him to scorn, as this was a new development, but at last were persuaded to go and hear for themselves. To their astonishment they found the tale was true, and music of the most ravishing description floated from the ruinous windows of the tower. They listened with bated breath, for never had they heard strains so sweet and sensuous. Soft and low came the music, with a rhythm like a dance, while feet within the tower could be heard distinctly, keeping time to the musicians. Then the music swelled and grew louder and louder, and eerie and uncanny, until it reached a riot and revelry, a perfect climax of devilry. For a short space there was silence, and once more the uncanny music began. Again they listened entranced, once more came a silence, and for the third time the music stole forth. One of the men could bear it no longer, and quietly approaching the door he put his hand upon the latch. Even as he moved there came a terrific crash of sound.

Utter silence followed. It was in broad daylight, and the three men searched the tower. It was completely empty.

In the dwelling-house of Knockshinnoch, near the haunted tower, there was a ghost that was seen of many. An old, old man, dressed in garments of an ancient cut, haunted the dark corners of lonely rooms. And many saw him and would have spoken to him, for he looked wistful and sad, but always as they approached him he faded into nothingness.

In Edinburgh a number of vaults are located beneath Niddry Street. They were built in the eighteenth century to support the street and make it more accessible to the high ridge of the Royal Mile, which runs down the spine of the hill on which the Old Town was built. The vaults are basically empty, but are one of the highlights on the various ghost tours that take place in the city centre. Various guides take visitors into the vaults, and during these visits a number of people have witnessed strange sights. The spectres witnessed are varied, and include a tall spirit of a man, whose clothing dates him to the eighteenth century. He sports knee-length leather boots. Scarier is the spirit of a woman dressed in white. She is quite young in appearance, but her body is covered with bloody wounds. A third ghost manifests as a gentleman of around forty years of age, not as tall as the first ghost, but who wears long leather boots like him. He also wears a leather apron that may indicate that he worked as a blacksmith, or in some other trade that involved a fire.

Previously mentioned in chapter six is the ghost of Sir George MacKenzie who is claimed to manifest in the vaults, as well as in Greyfriars kirkyard where he is buried. An American visitor who was taking part in one of the ghost tours entered the vaults. Rather sceptical of the tales of ghosts, she soon changed her mind when she experienced what she described as a strange evil presence in the vault. This was attributed to MacKenzie.

9

Country Haunts

Tales of ghosts appearing along roads are legion in Scotland. There are many accounts of ghostly cars and other vehicles being sighted on the roads. Hundreds of people recount having seen a vehicle driving in the near distance, coming towards them. The driver slows down, expecting to see the vehicle as he turns a corner, but when he does so there is nothing to be seen. What is more surprising is the fact that there is nowhere for the vehicle to have gone, such as into a side road or even through a gate into a field. Understandably, the driver is often left rather shaken after such incidents.

Some accounts given by drivers claim that they had to swerve, slow down or stop in order to avoid people crossing the road in front of them. When they emerge shaken from their cars they discover that there is no one to be seen. One of these sightings took place on a minor road near Leven in Fife in the winter of 1995–6. A motorist was driving along when he spotted what he thought were two miners making their way across the road. The driver acted quickly to avoid the pedestrians, after which he stopped the car to give them a piece of his mind. However, when he got up out of the driver's seat, he was stunned to find that there was no one around. They seemed to have vanished into thin air. Ann Anderson, a psychic investigator from Glenrothes, investigated the spot where the apparition was seen, but was unable to confirm who the miners might have been.

In 1953 David Campbell and his wife were travelling along the Cockbridge to Tomintoul road. They were in the area on business, and were lodging at a hotel in Grantown on Spey. It was early evening as they drove up the steep hill from Cockbridge, crossing one of the highest public roads in Scotland. Suddenly David became aware of steering problems, and after stopping discovered that this was due to a flat tyre. He took out the spare wheel from the boot and was in the process of changing it when he became aware of an old woman walking along the road. She came up to him and asked if she could be of any assistance. David looked at the frail old woman, who was dressed in a long skirt and head-scarf, and thanked her for her offer, but explained that he was nearly finished and would soon be on his way. The woman then carried on down the road. David finished changing the wheel, put his tools away, and started up the engine once more.

Discussing the old woman with his wife, he remarked that it was really friendly of her to offer some help, but he wondered whether or not she would have been up to it. His wife mentioned that she had not seen the woman as they drove along, but thought that it would be a kind gesture if they offered her a lift to Tomintoul, or wherever she was heading. They drove along the road quite slowly in order to stop when they caught her up, but she was nowhere to be seen. It was still light, being the summer, but after driving half a mile or more they had still not passed her. They stopped in order to look over the surrounding moor just in case she was there, but could not find her. She never did turn up.

A similar tale dates back to the late nineteenth century. Writing in *Gairloch* in 1886, John Dixon related that he had met a young man two years previously who had witnessed a phantom traveller. The lad had been walking along the road on a dark night when a figure came up alongside him. The lad spoke to the figure but there was no response. It seemed to just disappear into the night. Although the lad was adamant that the figure was some form of spectre, Dixon was less

218

convinced, noting that as there was no reply the lad considered this as 'proof positive of the ghostly nature of the appearance!'

An even older haunting took place on 11 January 1797. Two men were making their way along a road near Keith in Banffshire on a moonlit night. They called in at a farm for a short period before resuming their journey. Within a few moments a loud wailing was heard, so loud that it attracted the attention of various people in the vicinity. No one was able to work out where the sound was coming from, but whilst the sound was audible, the light from the moon seemed to shine brighter than anyone had ever experienced before.

Soon people became aware of smoke billowing from the slopes of the Hill of Auchinachie. As they looked towards the hill, the bright moonlight meant that they were able to discern that the smoke came from Cottertown croft. Dozens of men ran to the cottage to try and douse the flames. Work went on long into the night, and when the fire was put out they discovered the burned bodies of George Milne and his daughter. The strange wailing and bright moonlight had attracted the people's attention to the fire, which was found out to be the climax to a robbery carried out by two strangers. They were never caught. The wailing, however, was thought to be some form of supernatural phenomenon associated with the murder.

On the outskirts of Pitlochry in Perthshire is a crossroads that has a long-standing reputation for its haunting. One of the country's greatest ghost authors, Elliott O'Donnell, was in the area when he witnessed something unusual. He had been cycling all day, and was returning to his digs in Pitlochry when he decided to halt at the crossroads to take in the setting sun. As he gazed towards the colourful sky he suddenly became aware that there seemed to be a shaft of light coming from the sky and lighting up the crossroads. The light was very strange and was most unlike anything he had ever seen before. Suddenly he noticed two men riding on a haycart. The horse had also witnessed the shaft of light, which had by now taken the form of some kind of spectre, and had halted by itself. The men on the cart became agitated, and seemed to indicate that they had witnessed the strange apparition before. As soon as they were able they had turned the horse and were riding furiously in the opposite direction.

O'Donnell was by now scared out of his wits, and got back on his bicycle and rode into Pitlochry. He related his experience to his landlady, Flora MacDonald, who had heard of similar sightings. She told him that the spectre had appeared a number of times and that he was quite right to flee the spot, for should the apparition touch anyone, they would die within a short period of time. She told him that near to the crossroads had been a small country-house known as Old White House. Sir Arthur Holkitt had occupied it at one time, but when he moved out the building became impossible to sell. It had a reputation for being haunted, for it was supposed to occupy the site of an old burial ground, and it was eventually demolished. Flora MacDonald reckoned that the ghost of the crossroads may have had something to do with the ancient cemetery.

On the outskirts of the Borders village of St Boswells is a minor road linking the village with the old ruined church and cemetery, which is all that is left of the former ancient village of St Boswells. The road, which is only half a mile in length, stretches from near Lessudden House in a south-easterly direction towards the old kirkyard. In the late nineteenth century, the number of sightings made along this road by different people was so great that the Society for Psychical Research regarded it as one of the most authentic spots for ghost sightings. John Lang, writing in *Highways and Byways in*

The Border in 1913, noted, 'I know some of the percipients who have seen him individually and collectively. There is no tradition about the origin of this harmless appearance, a vision of a dream of the dead: walking 'in that sleep of death'.'

In 1874 a nine-year-old girl witnessed a ghost on this road. She lived at Benrig and was making her way home from the village. The road is straight for the first few hundred yards, and the girl spotted an old man dressed in black walking in front of her. However, as he turned the sharp corner on the road, he disappeared without any explanation.

Around 1880 a local farmer used the road as a short-cut into St Boswells. He was riding in a gig towards the village when he became aware of a figure on the road in front of him. The road being narrow, he slowed down ready to inch past. As he did so he noticed that the man was elderly, and that he wore the clothing of a minister from the previous century. A few yards after passing him the farmer decided to stop and offer him a lift into the village. As he turned round, however, the colour in his face drained when he realized that the figure had instantly disappeared.

On 14 August 1894 Mary Irvine, a school

governess, was walking along the road mid-afternoon. She suddenly spotted a man dressed in black, and again she described him as wearing clothes associated with a minister of the previous century, clothes from perhaps 150 years earlier. The manifestation was talking to a man who was working by the roadside, cutting the hedge. As Miss Irvine caught up with the hedger she noticed the minister had gone. She asked the hedger who the man had been, but he replied that he had been talking to no one, and had seen nobody for more than an hour.

The Scott sisters who lived at Lessudden House witnessed many of the sightings. They were the unmarried daughters of Robert Scott of Raeburn and Lessudden and Louisa Campbell. Matilda Wishart Scott (1863–1949) was walking along the road towards Lessudden on the afternoon of Sunday, 7 May 1892. She had probably taken a circular tour from the house, of which a number are possible. In any case, she was walking alone when she took the notion to sprint. As she did so, she became aware of a figure in the distance in front of her. She reckoned that it would be best to walk, for in those days it was still frowned upon to work or exercise on the sabbath. She watched the man in front of her, but as he rounded a corner she was shocked to see him disappear before her very eyes. Matilda knew that he had not left the road, for it was bordered by a thick beech hedge, but she could not work out where he had gone.

As she rounded the corner herself, she spotted her sister, Louisa (1868–1968), in the distance. Louisa was just as shocked as Matilda, and when they were close enough to converse, she asked Matilda who the man was and where he had disappeared. It was then that fear gripped them as they realized they had both witnessed the same spectre from different locations.

On another occasion, just two months later, Matilda and another sister, Susan Horsburgh Scott (1863–1949), were making their way together along the road. Suddenly Matilda became aware of a figure in black in the distance, and this time she was determined to find out whom the person was. She made her way towards him as fast as she could, and as she came up next to him she slowed down. She was able to see that he wore black clothing, from his coat to his breeches. He wore a white cravat about his neck and an unusual low-crowned hat on his head. She described his face as being deathly pale. As she took this in, however, 'he faded away to the bank on our right,' according to her account. Matilda went to the spot where he vanished but there was nothing to indicate that he had been there.

Matilda and Susan saw the ghost one more time. They had been picking wild strawberries from the roadside when they were disturbed by a thud coming from behind them. When they turned round they were amazed to see the old man in black. This time Matilda did not have any strength to face the spirit, for its sallow face and expression had put the fear of death into her. As she and Susan clung together they were even more horror-stricken to see the spectre fade away before their very eyes. They then ran as fast as they could back to Lessudden House. Matilda is known to have seen the spirit on at least four other occasions. These were in July 1893, August 1898, July 1900 and August 1900. On each occasion the spirit appeared as they walked along this road, either to or from Benrig.

Speculation about the identity of the Benrig Ghost (as the spectre soon became known) was rife in the area. It was claimed that it was the restless spirit of a minister who had murdered his housekeeper for some reason. This was said to have happened a century and a half earlier (around 1750), but research into the ministers of the period has proved no link. In any case, sightings of the ghost seem to have stopped in 1900.

Many remote moors and hillsides through-out Scotland have a reputation for being haunted. Arnish Moor on the island of Lewis has long been associated with ghosts. The moor stretches west from Stornoway Harbour to the main road that joins Stornoway itself with Tarbert on Harris. At some time in the eighteenth century two men were making their way across the moor, perhaps heading for Leurbost or some other township. For some reason the two men fell out, and in the ensuing brawl one of them was killed. Taking fright at his actions, the other man decided to bury his friend's body on the moor. When he arrived at his destination he told his family that he had become separated from his friend on the road and was unable to find him again.

Within weeks of the murder other travellers began reporting strange sightings on the moor. Some saw the figure of a man walking along the road, others were just sure that they were being followed. Those who witnessed the spectre described him as wearing a coat and woollen stockings up to his knees. The sightings of the stranger continued to appear up until the 1960s. All sightings seem to have ceased in 1964, for in that year the corpse of the murdered man was discovered buried in the peat. The acid soil had preserved much of the body, and his clothing was in good condition and very similar to the garments described by the witnesses.

Mervyn Hendry was working as a game-keeper on one of Perthshire's many sporting estates. One day he was out on the hill, checking up on the game and preparing for the season ahead. At lunchtime he stopped for a rest on a pleasant spot of heather near to a track that was used by shooters to reach the upper slopes. As he sat eating his lunch a mist suddenly dropped, spreading its hoary fingers around him. Suddenly, through the mist, he was aware of a group of tinkers or travelling people making their way up the hillside. They were travelling at right angles to the roadway, but made their way steadily across the heather and disappeared into the mist behind him. The party comprised horses and old-fashioned caravans, and the gamekeeper was quite impressed by this group of gypsies who seemed to adhere to the traditional ways. Thinking that the route chosen by the tinkers was rather obscure, he continued with his lunch. Within a short time the mist swirled up into the sky again and once more he had a clear view of the hillside. As he searched for the tinkers' caravans he discovered that they were nowhere to be seen, despite the vast panorama afforded from where he stood. The tinkers had not had sufficient time to get out of sight. It was only then that he realized that what he saw had been some form of ghostly traffic. At a later date, looking at old maps of the estate, he discovered that the route taken by the entourage followed the line of an ancient track no longer visible on the ground.

A number of rural locations in Aberdeenshire are home to manifestations of one sort or another. At West Knock farm, which is near to Stuartfield village, a Green Lady haunts a hollow in the ground. Who she was and why she decided to frequent this spot is not known.

Near by, at Winnyslap, an old cart-track is the spirit home of a female figure. The story relates that she was the daughter of a farmer and was engaged to be married in the near future. On the evening before the wedding she was walking down the cart track when a figure appeared from the bushes and lunged at her from behind. A short tussle ensued, and the attacker ran off across the fields leaving her lifeless body by the roadside. It was said that the groom-to-be had fallen out of love with his fiancée and could not bring himself to call off the wedding. Murder was the only way he could think of to avoid getting married.

In the first quarter of the nineteenth century, an old man by the name of Alasdair MacIain MacEarchair lived at the Craig of Gairloch in Wester Ross. He left his cottage one day to gather bog fir for the fire. This could be found in the peat bogs near his home. As he was gathering the firewood he suddenly became aware of a tall man watching him. He had fair hair and wore a traditional highland belted plaid. The man had twelve others in attendance, and all were dressed in a similar manner. The plaids were all of MacKenzie tartan. The tall man asked Alasdair, 'How fare the Gairloch family?' Alasdair told him that they were all well. On hearing this news the thirteen men disappeared silently, with only the effects of a strange wind being apparent. Alasdair was convinced that he had witnessed the ghost of Hector Roy MacKenzie, the first MacKenzie laird of Gairloch. It was he who established that clan in the west of the county — previously the land belonged to the MacLeods.

An old roadway in Midlothian is haunted by a galloping horseman. The roadway, which was at one time an important route linking Dalkeith and Peebles, is now little more than a byroad passing the old hamlet of Mount Lothian, before degenerating into a moorland track as it crosses the Cockmuir. It is said that in the late nineteenth century a man who worked on one of the local farms used to secretly borrow his master's horse so that he could ride the seven miles to Eddleston village, where he was wooing a young woman. Each evening he rode back to the farm and returned the horse to the stable before it was missed.

One night, as the farm labourer was riding across the moor, he heard the sound of a man groaning with pain. In the distance he spotted an upturned horse and cart, its load of limestone from the Mount Lothian quarries scattered across the road. The labourer decided that he would avoid the accident, for he was keen to see his girlfriend and did not want to be caught borrowing the horse. Turning his head the other way, he rode past the man who was calling for help.

Later that night, as he came back home, his heart was in his mouth as he came towards the site of the accident. The cart was still there, but the injured man made less noise. Again the labourer did not wish to be caught with the horse, so he passed on by. However, the man trapped beneath the cart recognized him this time. Next morning a search was sent out to find the missing man. When they came across him and his cart he was in the last throes of life. However, just before he died, he was able to tell the search party of the labourer and how he had avoided assisting him twice. Word spread like wildfire about this, and within days no one would talk to him. He was sacked from his job, and his girlfriend disowned him. Shortly afterwards he disappeared, and within a few days his corpse was found on the moors thereabouts. Some say he had taken his own life in a fit of remorse. Others think that friends of the injured man killed him. Whatever happened, it is said that the ghosts of him and his horse frequent the open countryside of Cauldhall and Cockmuir moors.

In Harta Corrie on the island of Skye is a huge boulder known as the Bloody Stone. This marks the site of a bloody battle that took place between the MacLeods and the MacDonalds in 1395. Since that time lonely travellers in the vicinity of the corrie have reported seeing the faint sight of ghostly warriors carrying on the fight.

There are numerous tales recorded from all over Scotland of phantom soldiers marching across moors or hillsides. In the 1830s or thereabouts, in the parish of Gairloch, a gardener, Donald MacLean, used to walk many miles between his home and place of employment, which was Inveran House. On a number of occasions as he walked either to or from work, he witnessed the sight of soldiers marching across the ridge of hills known as Creag Ruadh and Creag Bhan. The soldiers were dressed in red uniforms, and it was noted that the vision became impressed deeply on MacLean's mind. He often recounted what he saw to his employer, Duncan MacRae, as well as to others. It was later realized that what Donald had seen was a vision of the Poolewe section of the Gairloch volunteers marching back and forth towards Inveran. These soldiers wore scarlet Highland doublets, hence Donald's vision of red uniforms.

A similar story is told of countless ships appearing in Little Loch Broom, a sea-loch on the north-west coast of Scotland. This took place in 1822, when most of the men folk had walked a number of miles to Loch Broom where the minister was holding communion. Most of the women and children who had been left behind saw the ships, which were so numerous that they almost covered the waters of the loch. As they gazed in wonder at the sight, the witnesses were concerned to see some soldiers disembark from the vessels, and make their way to the shore. So close were the figures that it was said that the women could see whom they represented. Some of the residents of the area were so perturbed by the sight that they took all their valuables from their homes and buried them, lest the soldiers raided their properties. Some of the women left the area and headed for the relative safety of their sheilings (traditional summer huts). However, the soldiers never came ashore, and the whole thing was explained as a mass occurrence of second sight.

Second sight is something that seems to be rather peculiar to Scotland. It occurs when someone witnesses something but discovers later that what they saw did not take place. At a later date, often years later, the very same vision is re-enacted, but this time for real. Second sight is something that was common among the highland people of Scotland, but even to this day there are people who claim to have the gift. In most cases individuals only witness some sight or other on one occasion, usually when some major event is being foretold. Those who seem to be able to use the skill on numerous occasions are known as 'seers', the Brahan Seer being one of the most famous examples.

The eminent geologist and writer, Hugh Miller, noted some examples of second sight in his *Scenes and Legends of the North of Scotland*. At the outbreak of the Napoleonic wars there were people in the Inverness area who witnessed soldiers marching on the moor south of the town. It was later discovered that the time these soldiers were seen matched exactly with the time the first battle took place.

Another example given by John Dixon in his *Gairloch*, published in 1886, is here repeated in full:

At the date of this story the blacksmith at Poolewe had his house and smithy where the Pool-house stable now stands. It was close by the east side of Poolewe bridge, from which the spectator can look down into the deep gloomy pool at which the River Ewe joins the brackish waters of Loch Ewe. The smith had a son, a boy, almost a young man; he was in sickly health at the time, and died shortly afterwards. The late Revd William Rose, Free Church minister of Aultbea and Poolewe, who died in April 1876, told me that one day the smith's son had walked over to Gairloch, and returning somewhat exhausted, came into his father's house (the door being open), and instantly sat down on the nearest chair. No sooner was he seated than he fell from the chair in a fainting fit. He presently came round, and on recovering consciousness the first thing he said to his family was, 'What are all these people on the bridge for?' They pointed out to him that there was no one on the bridge. He then told them that as he had approached the bridge he had seen it crowded with people, that he had had to push his way through them and that he had felt very much frightened. Those members of the smith's household who were at home had seen no one on the bridge; the doors and windows of the house faced the bridge, and were not thirty yards from it, so that no individuals, much less a crowd, could have been on the bridge without the family having noticed them. The following day, the 3rd October 1860, was a day that will never be forgotten by those who witnessed its terrible events. A number of open boats with their crews were at the head of Loch Ewe near Boor, Cliff House, and Poolewe, setting nets for herrings, when a storm suddenly came on, far exceeding in violence any other storm before or since, so far as those now living remember. A hurricane sprang up from the west-north-west, of such extraordinary force as actually to lift boats and their crews from the water, and in one or two cases to overturn the boats. Happily most of the men clung to their boats, and were soon washed ashore.

One boat was carried rapidly past the point called Ploc-ard, by Inverewe House. As she was passing close to some big stones one of her crew jumped out on to a rock, but was washed off and drowned. In another boat, opposite Cliff House, there were four men; the boat was capsized and three of the men were drowned; the fourth had tied himself to the boat, which came ashore by Cliff House; he was taken to the house, and restoratives being applied soon recovered. About a score of the boats ran into the pool under Poolewe bridge. And thus the vision of the smith's son was fulfilled, for at the very hour at which he had crossed the bridge on the preceding day, a multitude of the fishermen's friends and relations, breathless with agonising anxiety, crowded the bridge and its approaches watching the arrival of the boats. The tide on this awful evening rose one hundred and fifty yards further up the shore and adjoining lands than on any other occasion remembered in the district. The bodies of the drowned men were recovered, and were buried in the Inverewe churchyard, where the date of this memorable storm is recorded on a gravestone over the remains of two of the men named William Urquhart and Donald Urquhart.

The area of East Kilbride known as St Leonard's was haunted by the spectre of Jenny Cameron. Jenny was born in Glen Dessarry in the Western Highlands in the early eighteenth century. She was a passionate Jacobite, and it is well known that she organized around three hundred of her fellow clansmen to attend the raising of the Prince's standard at Glenfinnan. After the defeat at the Battle of Culloden in 1746, Jenny was forced to leave her homeland and eventually settled at a village known as East Kilbride. There she ran a school for orphans and managed to earn sufficient funds to purchase a small estate named Blacklaw. When she died in 1772 the locals were unable to accede to her last wish and bury her in Glen Dessarry, due to the distance. Instead, she was laid to rest in a grave on her own land.

The grave was left for a couple of centuries, but in the 1960s, when East Kilbride was developed as one of Scotland's new towns, it was surrounded by a golf course. As soon as it opened, many golfers reported seeing some form of glowing light in the vicinity of the grave. Some felt that this was Jenny's spirit, upset at not being allowed to lie in peace in her home countryside. The site of the golf course has since been developed for housing, though the area around the grave has been preserved as a play park. In 1995 a new memorial was erected there as part of the 250th anniversary of the Jacobite rising. The spirit of Jenny seems to have settled in recent years.

In a remote glen of upper Clydesdale stand the ruins of what is known as Windgate House, or Hall. This building was for many years abandoned, the ruins overgrown. Earlier accounts of the building reported a stone vault of some sort, hence the locals calling the ruins 'The Vaults', but this collapsed many years ago, and even in 1924 'the arch had completely collapsed and filled up the interior, but in places the first two or three courses of its springing still remained', according to A. MacCallum Scott, writing in *Clydesdale*. For many years it was assumed that this building had been some form of fortified castle, or tower house, but recent excavations have proved that it was a bastle house — that is, a fortified building erected during the time of the Border reivers. The ruins have since been stabilized.

MacCallum Scott later quoted a shepherd that he met on his perambulations:

A neighbour shepherd once came doon by that spot wi' his dog at mirk. He saw twa figures standing on the ruin but when he

238

got up to it they had disappeared. His dog was cowed and would not leave his heel a' the way home. It is not for me to say they were ghosts. You can take what meaning you like from it, but it was a curious occurrence.

Other accounts claim that the two figures manifested as a young couple in Victorian garb. It is claimed that they only appear when something serious is about to happen to the family who own Lamington House. Lamington House occupies the site of an ancient castle, and was for centuries owned by the Baillie family. The *Statistical Account* of the parish (written at the end of the eighteenth century) claims that Windgate was 'built at a remote period by the laird of Lammingtoune, at a time when a feud subsisted between him and the laird of Symington'. The laird of Symington had built Fatlips Castle on the side of Tinto in order to spy on his neighbour, whereupon the laird of Lamington built Windgate House in a remote glen on his estate to give him privacy.

It is quite a coincidence to discover that a granddaughter of the witness who saw the Windgate ghosts married Tam Ward, the archaeologist responsible for excavating and stabilizing the ruins. During the excavation he spent some time camped in the vicinity, but he was pleased to tell me that he never experienced anything untoward. They joked as they dug at the ruins what they would do if they found two skeletons, but the only bones that they found belonged to sheep. Nevertheless, he told me that the sheepdog who was with the shepherd that day refused to pass through that part of the glen again, instead taking a much more strenuous route round the neighbouring hilltops.

10

Mansion Manifestations

Many of Scotland's country houses have tales of ghosts frequenting them. Hundreds of these old mansions occupy the site of earlier castles, and the ghosts that haunt these houses are often thought to have originated in the older building. Many other spectres however, are connected with the more modern building, and in many cases the earthly being that the spirit represents is known.

Floors Castle is one of the largest country houses in Scotland. The Duke of Roxburghe owns it, and it dates from 1721. It was built west of Kelso, to the plans of William Adam, for the first duke. Two spirits are said to haunt the grounds, although sightings of them are rarely, if ever, made. The first haunting occurs near to the entrance, in the large courtyard between the mansion's wings. The presence of the estate gardener has often been felt here, though his spectre seems never to be seen. A number of people walking across the gravel forecourt have felt shivers down their neck as they stood on the freshly-raked stones, as though the gardener were berating them for disturbing his handiwork.

The second spirit at Floors is also located outside the building. Immediately to the south-east of the castle, on the flat holm by the side of the River Tweed, is an old holly tree that is said to date from the fifteenth century. This marks the spot where James II was killed on 3 August 1460, when the barrel of his cannon burst during the siege of Roxburgh Castle. Fragmentary ruins of the castle rise up on the other side of the river from here, crowning a mound above the River Teviot. The ghost is probably not of the king himself, however, for it appears as a horseman riding across the fields here.

Houndwood House is an old castellated mansion, standing in the valley of the Eye Water, four miles from Ayton in Berwickshire. The house incorporates an older tower house and it is claimed that part of the vaulted ground floor dates from the twelfth century. The bones of monks who formerly owned this as a hunting lodge are said to exist in the cellars. In the nineteenth century there were stories associating the house with a ghost named 'Chappie'. This was thought to be the manifestation of a child. She is sometimes heard wailing and weeping within the building, but more often than not is responsible for knocking at doors and windows. A number of residents in the house have heard these sounds at the windows, even on upper floors. Scared out of their wits, those fearless enough to go to the window find that no one is there, and that nothing on the outside could be responsible for the sounds.

Another spectre is said to be responsible for heavy footsteps that have been heard coming from empty rooms on the floor above. Other inexplicable sounds have been attributed to it, from knocking on walls and doors, to heavy breathing and groans. Tradition states that at some point in its history, some soldiers killed a man here. His corpse was then cut in half for some unknown reason. The apparition of the lower half of a male body has been witnessed in the grounds surrounding the house. Those who have seen it state that the legs are wearing what looks like riding breeches.

A third spirit at Houndwood has been heard on occasion. Some folk claim that they have heard the sound of horses riding in the woods on either side of the burn, but on closer inspection have discovered that no horses, nor hoofprints, can be seen. The sound of horses has also been reported in the vaulted passage on the lower floor of the house. It is claimed that this sound comes from the ghostly apparition of Mary Queen of Scots' horse. That she was in fact here was confirmed by the discovery in 1868 of her wedding ring, found among the roots of a tree that had blown over in the garden.

Old Linthill House is a rather fine old Border mansion standing on a brae above the Eye Water, one mile from Eyemouth. The house has a tragic tale associated with it. The butler murdered the old woman who lived in the house and proceeded to steal her belongings. However, as in all good horror movies, the woman was not totally dead and she managed to raise the alarm. The butler jumped from the first floor window but broke his leg in the fall. He was later captured and hanged. At Old Linthill there is a spot on the wainscoting where the old woman's bloodied hand left marks that have never been possible to remove.

Yet the strange sounds that are heard at Old Linthill are not associated with the murder, and the tale with which they are associated has long since been forgotten. There is an upper room in the house in which the sound of a thud on the floor is sometimes heard. It is usually preceded by the sound of an invisible vehicle making its way up the drive to the house and footsteps making their way to the room. On investigation nothing is ever seen.

Buchanan Castle was a rather grand baronial building, standing in extensive parklands at the southern end of Loch Lomond. It replaced an older castle gutted by fire in 1850, but the new castle is now itself a rather grand ruin and its parkland laid out as a golf course. The castle was said to be haunted whilst it was still occupied, and in the summer evenings strange sounds can still be heard. No actual ghost seems to have been seen, but many people have experienced the sounds. These tend to sound rather like a gasp, as though some unseen spirit has witnessed a tragic event. What this may have been or when it may have taken place has not been handed down in traditional tales.

The sounds at Buchanan are usually reported after eleven o'clock at night, and those who know about country life state that they were definitely not made by animals or birds. One such person was able to record the sounds. On another occasion two men were exploring the ruins with the aid of a strong torch. On the second floor of the building the light mysteriously went out, and they thought at first that they must have knocked the torch and broken the filament in the bulb. However, when they returned to the floor below the torchlight came back on again, and worked perfectly thereafter.

Not too far from Buchanan is Loch Lomond Youth Hostel. This is located in the mansion house of Auchendennan, which lies on the west side of the loch. In the tower there is a room where the manifestation of a girl has been seen walking across it a number of times. Who she was is not known. At one time there were pictures on the panels in the girl's room but workmen burned these off. Carol Hutchins, warden at the hostel for a time, states that they miraculously reappeared within a short time.

Dalzell House at Motherwell in Lanarkshire is an old baronial mansion, parts of which date from the sixteenth century. In recent years it has been divided into smaller houses, all of which seem to be haunted. There are at least four ghosts here, and each one is described by a different colour. They seem to keep themselves to a particular part of the house, and all are distinguished by their own characteristics.

The White Lady haunts Dalzell's battlements. The earthly being that this spirit represents is said to be a former servant girl employed at the house. She fell pregnant whilst unmarried, and to prevent any embarrassment for herself and her parents, decided to jump to her death from the parapet.

Some folk say that Dalzell's Grey Lady was a nurse in life. The north wing of the house was used as a hospital during the First World War and it is thought that the ghost dates from that time. Why the ghost haunts the building is not known, for there are no known accounts of any nurse being killed or dying in the house at that time. In any case, the manifestation usually wears a nurse's uniform typical of the period.

The Brown Lady is usually witnessed in what was the nursery at Dalzell. Of her appearances, little is known.

The Green Lady at Dalzell usually manifests in the Green Bedroom, although there have also been sightings in the Piper's Gallery. Many of the witnesses who have seen this spirit are first aware of something when they smell a rather strong perfume. Soon after becoming aware of the aroma, and looking around to see where it may have come from, they usually catch a glimpse of the Green Lady out of the corner of their eye.

There have also been strange sounds experienced at Dalzell House. These vary from footsteps and knocking sounds to thuds and quiet music. At other times flashing lamps have been spotted coming from windows of rooms that are known to be empty and dark at the time.

On the edge of the Ayrshire town of Irvine stand the ruins of Eglinton Castle. This was a rather grand country house built between 1796 and 1802 to the plans of John Paterson for the Earl of Eglinton. Today the ruins form the centrepiece of a large country park. In 1996 two men were in the grounds when they spotted the face of an old man staring at them from one of the glassless windows in the old tower. The building is usually closed, and the men knew this at the time they witnessed the face. They turned to walk away but within seconds heard the rattling of the iron gate that locks the structure. Terrified, they ran as fast as they could, but the spectre pursued them. It seemed to have a large hood over its head, and Gary Devine claimed that he could feel something tugging at his back as he ran. His friend, Brian Cairney, stated that the ghost seemed to hover above them. 'I have never been so scared in my life,' he said. 'Even now when I think about it, it makes the hairs on the back of my neck stand on end.'

The hooded man seemed to be a new spectre at Eglinton Castle. Earlier witnesses claim to have seen a White Lady and a Grey

Lady, but who any of the spirits may have been in life is not known.

Liberton House stands within the suburbs of Edinburgh. An old building, it dates from 1680 but was gutted by fire around 1990. Restoration work followed to create a rather fine home. Liberton is home to a ghost that has been photographed. A reporter and photographer from the *Scotsman* called at the house in 1936, when it was subject to an earlier restoration. When the photograph was developed, the photographer was astounded when the shape of a human appeared standing in the porch. The figure was definitely not there when the picture was being taken. The spirit was of a large person, the face looking rather sinister. And yet the features were quite distinguished, the smile being likened to that of the Mona Lisa.

The porch was demolished in the most recent restoration work, but the ghost still seems to haunt the building. For no apparent reason electrical appliances seem to be able to switch themselves on and off. One morning the owner entered a room to discover a fan heater burning away, when she knew for definite that it had been switched off the previous evening. Burglar alarms go off when nothing earthly has disturbed them, and appliances in the kitchen seem to operate by themselves.

Saltoun Hall in East Lothian is a fine mansion of 1817, which incorporates an old castle. Long a seat of the Abernethy family, who held the title of Lord Saltoun, the Fletchers later owned it. Today it is subdivided into flats. A Grey Lady is said to haunt the castle but little is known about her.

Grangemuir House stood in the parish of Anstruther Wester in Fife. It had a long-standing reputation for being haunted by a ghostly female named Buff Barefoot. Her story was one of great sadness. As an infant she was left in a basket at the door of Grizel Miller's inn, which was located near St Monans harbour. Grizel took the basket in and opened up the blankets to reveal a beautiful baby girl. Buried in amongst the covers was a small bag that contained some gold coins. Grizel decided to bring the child up in her home. She grew into a beautiful young woman, but she preferred to wear neither shoes nor stockings, and earned the epithet 'Buff Barefoot'.

One day a relative of the Grangemuir family arrived at the house on a visit. He lived in the Border countryside, where he was renowned as a reiver. The visitor made his way to Newark Castle where he intended paying a social call, but spotted Buff Barefoot, who worked there as a maid. The reiver fell for her beauty, but by this time Buff had plighted her troth to a sailor who happened to be away at the time. The reiver tried to persuade her to go with him, but she steadfastly refused.

The sailor returned to St Monans harbour and went to the Doocot Hill to meet his fiancée. It was early evening and the sun was setting beyond Largo Law. Soon the villagers were disturbed by screams coming from the Doocot Hill. Some rushed to see what was wrong, and spotted the sailor running away. Near the doocot (dovecote) the body of Buff Barefoot was discovered lying motionless. She was dead.

The sailor, witnessed fleeing the site, was apprehended and held in Newark's dungeon. The Border reiver was later so overcome by remorse that he committed suicide. Just what happened that night has never been fully understood. However, since that time the ghost of Buff Barefoot has been seen in Grangemuir House. At the start the owners were often awoken during the night by the sound of bare feet stomping through the building. Others actually witnessed the spectre of Buff Barefoot, and within a short time the house was abandoned, the owners terrified to stay there. The building began to fall into ruin and eventually it was demolished. It was made sure that all of the stones were dumped and not reused, for fear of transferring the spirit to another building. A later Grangemuir House, built in 1807, occupies the site.

Kingcausie House stands near to the southern Deeside Road, west of Aberdeen. It has long been a seat of the Irvine family, for a time Irvine-Boswell and now Irvine-Fortescue. An old tower is incorporated in what is really a modern mansion. During the Christmas holidays of 1836 the family had grouped together to enjoy the festivities. John Irvine-Boswell and his wife had invited his nephew's family to the house. Charles Maitland Christie of Durie and his wife brought along their toddler, James Turner Christie.

The little boy was with his nanny on the upstairs landing. He kept pestering her to hold him up so that he could look over the banister. Eventually she gave in, but as she held the lad up he began to wriggle and break free of her grasp. He fell into the stairwell, plunging down the equivalent height of thirty-nine steps to the hall below. His nanny screamed in terror, attracting the family's attention, but when they arrived in the hall the little lad was dead. Only twenty-two months old, he was buried in the family plot in the old Maryculter burial ground by the side of the Dee.

Since that time the family have heard the sound of a youngster's feet running along the upper landing during the night. This has continued until recent times, and has been heard by various members of the family.

An unknown spectre haunts another room at Kingcausie. This is known as the 'Chinese Room' because of its furnishings. William Irvine-Fortescue claimed that the room was evil and, on two separate occasions as he lay in bed, woke up when the bedclothes suddenly rose into the air and dropped back down again. No one else was present on each occasion, and he never did work out what was responsible for this strange happening. On another occasion the same thing happened to two sisters who shared the bed. William's brother was awakened one night in 1952 to the sound of heavy banging on his bedroom door. No one else in the house had heard anything.

The spirit at Haddo House in Aberdeenshire dates back to 1909 when Lord Archibald Gordon was killed in a car crash. He was the youngest son of the 7th Earl of

Aberdeen (later to be created 1st Marquis of Aberdeen and Temair). His spirit has appeared a number of times in the Premier's Bedroom, named after the 4th Earl who was Prime Minister of Great Britain between December 1852 and January 1855. One of those who saw him was an aunt of Lady Aberdeen. She did not know who she was witnessing at the time, but was later able to describe the figure as rather young-looking, wearing a Norfolk jacket and with reddish golden-coloured hair. This haunting took place in the 1950s, but the family were able to confirm the likeness to Lord Archibald. A later sighting was confirmed as Lord Archibald when the witness looked at a portrait of the dead lord.

It is not only the ghost of the Marquis's son that causes unease at Haddo. On some occasions guests have complained that they were unable to sleep due to the horses in the stable next door. Only when it was explained to them that the stables that formerly occupied the north wing had not been there since it was converted in the late nineteenth century into a library, chapel and other rooms, did they realize that they must have heard something from the past.

Leith Hall is now a property of the National Trust for Scotland. It stands in remote countryside at Kennethmont, at the west end of Aberdeenshire. The house is built round a courtyard, but it was built in stages over the years, extending what was an old tower house. Today it is a delightful confection of pepper-pot turrets and towers.

There seem to be two different ghosts that haunt Leith Hall. The first is of a man who looks as though he is in hospital, having bandages tied around his head. It is reckoned that this manifestation represents John Leith, who died in 1763. He was the fourth Leith of Leith Hall, succeeding his father at the age of five. He later married Harriot Steuart and made a number of improvements to the house. However, three days before Christmas 1763 he rode from the house to Aberdeen where he was going to dine with friends. The dinner went well enough, then the claret started to flow rather too freely. Soon the men were arguing about the standard of their estate produce. Leith was accused of contaminating the meal produced there, a charge that he vehemently denied. Tempers flared, and soon there was a scuffle in the middle of the room. It is not known exactly just what happened next. A duel may have been organized, or else Leith was set upon, but he was shot through the head in the city's Castlegate. He died on Christmas Day. John

Leith was only thirty-two. His wife was pregnant at the time, and later gave birth to a son, but he survived for only one year.

In the late 1960s Barrie Gaunt and his wife, American novelist Elizabeth Byrd, tenanted Leith Hall. One night Elizabeth found that she was having difficulty sleeping in the master bedroom. She dozed on and off, and on one occasion awoke to witness John Leith standing between the foot of the four-poster bed and the dressing table. He sported a beard and was dressed in highland garb. Elizabeth screamed, and as she stared in disbelief he slowly faded away. Elizabeth was later able to identify the spirit from a portrait that hangs in the house, although it depicts Leith as clean-shaven.

Scottish novelist Alanna Knight and her husband Alistair spent a night at Leith Hall as guests of the Gaunts. It proved to be one of the most frightening nights they have ever experienced. Alanna and Alistair were awakened at the same time and felt as though there was someone else in the room. Alistair experienced the sensation of someone staring down closely at his face as he lay on the bed, as if the spirit was trying to see who was sleeping there.

The second haunting at Leith Hall is harder to explain. A number of guests staying at the house have reported hearing the sounds of a party taking place elsewhere in the house. Doors are heard banging and footsteps are heard in corridors. The sounds of a woman laughing are heard, and sometimes pipe-playing. Guests at the house in 1968 reported this strange experience, but there was no one else staying in the house at the time, and certainly no party taking place. On other occasions the smell of incense has been reported in various rooms throughout the house. Barrie Gaunt saw the spectre of a woman, dressed in the Victorian style, one day. She was acting rather surreptitiously.

Aden House in Aberdeenshire is now a roofless shell, and stands in the centre of an estate that is now a country park. The Russell family, who acquired it in the late eighteenth century, owned the house. The second laird had a daughter who fell in love with a footman who worked for her father. The friendship was discovered and the daughter was banned from seeing him again. Undaunted, the footman found himself a ladder and during the night made his way to the mansion house. Using the ladder he climbed up to her window and attracted her attention. She readily agreed to marry him, and both eloped off into the night. The daughter was discovered to be missing the next morning. From that time on the ghost of the young lady haunted the first floor room at Aden. This took place around 1810–20. Whether or not she had actually died is not known. A later occupier of the room discovered that she could not sleep for the haunting, and eventually the owner of the house had the room divided by a false wall, shutting off that part of it that was haunted. The 'hidden corridor' behind the wall was the subject of much speculation in later years.

Aden is said to be the home of another two spirits. When a photograph was taken of the drive leading from the house towards the village of Old Deer, a strange female figure appeared when the film was developed. The photographer was near to the old ice-house when the picture was taken and no person was in the frame when the picture was exposed. The female that appeared was dressed in what appears to be Victorian-style clothing, but who she was in life is not known. The third ghost at Aden manifests as a phantom monk. This ghost seems to appear very irregularly. Some folk say that Aden House and its immediate policies occupy the site of the original abbey of Deer, hence the monk.

Duff House, a rather fine William Adam

mansion house, stands on the edge of the ancient Royal Burgh of Banff. The house dates from 1735–41 and was erected for the First Earl of Fife. The house is home to a Green Lady. It is claimed that she walks through the rooms of the four-square house, though the present owners, Historic Scotland, tend to deny her existence. From what period she originates is not known. Perhaps she was one of the Duff women, or else she may have been a nurse who worked in the house during the time it operated as a sanatorium.

A small country house now surrounded by the suburbs of Inverness is claimed to be haunted by the spirit of a former owner. Culcabock House stands to the east of the town centre of the Highlands' capital, and part of it dates from 1532. Owned by the Grants of Glenmoriston, in 1645 the owner was renowned for his love of gambling. So severe were his debts that he decided to play cards to try and pay them off. Things got so bad that he was forced to put up the house as one of his bets, but unfortunately for him he lost. Having lost his mansion, he returned to the house to haunt the room where the ill-fated game took place. The ghost at Culcabock appears on very few occasions. Some say that he only appears to Grants, and only if that person is ready to take part in a battle — so the chances of seeing this spirit are very slim!

Auchinvole House is quite an old mansion standing to the south of Kilsyth, in what is now East Dunbartonshire. Part of the house incorporates an old tower house, and in an upper window the ghostly face of a beautiful woman has been reported. It is said that the spirit belongs to a daughter of the house who was engaged to be married. Her fiancé was tragically murdered before the ceremony could take place, and the girl is thought to have died soon after of a broken heart. Her spirit would gaze thereafter from her room to the spot where her fiancé was buried, longing for his return.

Craighall Rattray is an old mansion standing on a high rock promontory above the River Ericht, near Blairgowrie in Perthshire. The house has been the seat of the Rattray chiefs for centuries, and when seen from a distance looks rather like a Rhineland château. At times, though, when the weather is closing in and the mist is swirling in the glen, the house looks rather sinister. When one sees it like this, it is not surprising to discover that Craighall is home to at least two spectres.

A Grey Lady has been seen a number of

times at Craighall. Who she represents is not known, but her spirit has haunted the house for some time. Even in recent years she has made regular appearances in various rooms. This spectre seems to force itself on top of sleeping people, causing them to awaken due to the great weight on top of them. This phenomenon has been reported in other haunted buildings. Lachie Rattray recalls awaking one night to find a heavy pressure on top of his chest. It was none other than the Grey Lady. He was able to struggle and wrestle himself free, after which the spectre disappeared.

Craighall Rattray has other strange phenomena recorded within it. Inexplicable sounds have been heard in various parts of the rambling mansion, from phantom footsteps in empty corridors to the sound of knocking on doors and walls. Many visitors report having sensed a feeling that they are being watched, but on further investigation there is never anyone to be seen. This eerie feeling seems to be particularly strong in the house's north passage.

One of Craighall's rooms is known as the North Room. This is located in the oldest part of the building, which has its roots as an ancient Scottish castle. Most strangers who enter this room suddenly experience the strange feeling of being drawn towards the window. Most describe this as being rather 'irresistible'. The reason for this is explained by the fact that a servant girl was said to have been thrown from this window. During the seventeenth century the house was visited by Cromwell's troops. The Rattrays had managed to escape, hiding themselves in various places about the house and its immediate vicinity. The soldiers found a servant lass, but she steadfastly refused to betray any of the family. Their temper growing, the soldiers took her to the window and threw her from the building. The window stands high above the cliff, and the girl fell to her death far below. Ever since that time it is said that tapping sounds are heard on the outside of this window, as though the spirit of the servant girl was trying to get back in.

Achindown is a fairly small mansion house standing near to the Kirkton of Barevan, itself a mile south of Cawdor in Nairnshire. The spirit of a youngish girl has been seen here, gathering flowers. She usually wears a blue dress and has brown hair flowing over her shoulders. According to tradition, this apparition is of Elspeth Munroe, daughter of Hamish Munroe, who occupied the house in the first half of the eighteenth century. She allegedly eloped with a shepherd who worked on the estate.

Why the spirit of Elspeth Munroe remains at Achindown is not known, for it seems more likely that the ghosts of her father and family would manifest there. In 1746, shortly after their defeat at Culloden at the hands of Butcher Cumberland, a number of Jacobites sought refuge at this house, which dates from around 1700. Hanoverian soldiers arrived at the door and commenced a search. They found the Jacobites huddling together in the basement. They were dragged from their hiding place and taken into the garden, where they were shot dead. Hamish Munroe was likewise dispatched for having hidden the Jacobites. Marks on the garden wall at Achindown are said to have been a result of bullets ricocheting off the masonry.

The island of Cara is a 163-acre island located to the south of the larger island of Gigha, itself located off the west coast of Kintyre. Cara House is a fairly large farmhouse that probably dates from 1733, having been built by the MacDonalds of Largie as the residence of their tacksman. The house is home to one of the many brownies that haunt buildings throughout Scotland. The traditional tale claims that the brownie is the spectre of one of the MacDonalds who was murdered by a Campbell. It is not known when this took place. The ghost is said to frequent the attic rooms of the two-storey building, but has been spotted elsewhere. Sightings of him were fairly common, and in 1909 MacDonald of Largie claimed that the spirit often appeared or was heard in his bedroom. He described the brownie as, 'A neat little man, dressed in brown, with a pointed beard'. It was said that when the laird himself (or the minister) arrived at Cara House, he would have to raise his hat to the ghost in order to keep him happy. At the southern end of the island, at the headland known as the Mull of Cara, is a rock formation known as the Brownie's Chair. Even the church at Ardminish on Gigha has a loft known as the Brownie's Gallery.

As with all brownies, the Cara brownie liked to help out the family. He was liable to wash and put away dirty dishes, or else help bring in the harvest. One day some of MacDonald's servants arrived at Cara House in order to collect some barrels of wine from the cellar. The men were aware of the brownie and joked that he should be there to help them. Suddenly they discovered that they were unable to move the casks up the planks of wood they had placed up the steps as ramps. Realizing that they had upset the brownie, they spoke out loud an apology. Within seconds the casks were rolling themselves up the plank, and not only that — they also made their way down to the anchorage and on board the boat.

On the mainland of Orkney, or Pomona, stands Skaill House, a rather fine seventeenth-century mansion. The oldest part was erected around 1625 for the Bishop of Orkney, George Graham, but it was extended to the south and north to create a lengthy group of linked buildings, distinguished by their corbie-stepped gables and linking walls. Skaill has been operating as a country house hotel since 1997. The house overlooks the Bay of Skaill, where the neolithic village of Skara Brae is located.

Skaill House is haunted by the spectre of an old woman that has appeared a number of times in different parts of the building. Who she was is not known. There have also been strange sounds of footsteps heard coming from empty rooms. Perhaps there is something in the fact that under the ownership of Henry William Scarth (between 1929 and 1972), human bones were found beneath the floor of the house. These were discovered when a flagged floor in the old hall was being replaced.

Within the flanking wings of Skaill House,

the present owner has created holiday flats. A number of visitors that have spent their holidays there often relate how they seem to be joined by uninvited guests. Dogs have also heard the strange sounds in the house, their hairs rising and claws gripping into the floor. Cleaners at the house left one of the holiday flats untouched because there were still guests present when they went to clean it. When they reported this to the owner he retorted that the holidaymakers had left earlier that day and the apartment should be empty. When they returned they discovered that the apartment was indeed vacant.

Windhouse on the Shetland island of Yell is a small country house that has been abandoned to the elements for some time, although the Royal Society for the Protection of Birds has proposals to restore it and sell it on. The house was originally erected in 1707 as a simple two-storey farmhouse, but around 1880 it was extended and remodelled. Castellated wings were added to create a home of some stature for these islands, but by the 1930s the house had been so neglected that it had fallen into ruin. Today it forms part of the RSPB's Lumbister bird sanctuary.

Four different ghosts have been reported at the house over the years. One of these spirits takes the form of a black dog, wandering along the corridors. A second spirit appears in the form of a young child; she was witnessed in what had been the kitchens of the house.

The third Windhouse ghost is that of a woman. She wears a silk dress, and from her appearance it has been surmised that she was a housekeeper here. Other accounts say that she was the mistress of the owner of the house. Her manifestation is usually witnessed on the stairs, and it is claimed that her earthly being died after falling down them and breaking her neck. Other people claim that an old woman who was being evicted from her croft at the beginning of the nineteenth century placed a curse on the house. She is said to have warned the laird that, 'Neither you nor your family will prosper, and one day the sheep will wander through the middle of your home.' The latter fact certainly came true, for the house has lost its windows and many of its doors.

Windhouse's fourth spectre is the most sinister. It appears as a heavily-built man who is able to walk through walls. Perhaps there were doors at these places prior to the 1880 reconstruction. One account has him appearing out of a hole in the ground. He appears wearing a dark cloak and hat, and some say that he was a pedlar who arrived at

Windhouse one day only to be murdered. During the rebuilding work in 1880 a skeleton of a male was discovered hidden in the building, and it has been surmised that it belonged to this ghost.

Windhouse's early lairds had some evil reputations. One of them was renowned for his ruthlessness in acquiring land, often swindling farmers out of their properties. He also tried to attack the local minister, and was imprisoned for murdering someone else. Claims that the body of a tax collector was discovered at the house cannot be proved, nor can the tale that states one of the labourers was murdered in a drunken brawl and buried outside the kitchen window. Nevertheless, Windhouse has long had an evil reputation, and the locals are said to be terrified of the house because of its spectres, making sure that they are nowhere near it after sunset.

Bibliography

Adams, Norman, *Haunted Neuk*
(Tolbooth Books, 1994)
— , *Haunted Valley* (Tolbooth Books, 1994)
— , *Haunted Scotland* (Mainstream, 1998)
Bardens, Dennis, *Ghosts & Hauntings*
(Zeus Press, 1965)
Barty, Alexander B., *History of Dunblane*
(Eneas Mackay, 1944)
Beveridge, David, *Between the Ochils and
the Forth* (William Blackwood, 1888)
Cameron, John, *The Parish of Campsie*
(D. MacLeod, 1892)
Coventry, Martin, *The Haunted Castles of
Scotland* (Goblinshead, 1996)
— , *Haunted Places of Scotland*
(Goblinshead, 1999)
— , *Scottish Ghosts and Bogles*
(Goblinshead, 2000)
Dixon, John H., *Gairloch*
(Co-operative Printing Co., 1886)
Fyall, Aitken, *St Monans*
(Pentland Press, 1999)
Halliday, Ron, *Paranormal Scotland*
(B&W Publishing, 2000)

Hannan, Thomas, *Famous Scottish Houses* (A&C Black, 1928)

Lang, Andrew & John, *Highways and Byways in the Border* (Macmillan, 1913)

Love, Dane, *Scottish Ghosts* (Robert Hale, 1995)

— , *The Auld Inns of Scotland* (Robert Hale, 1997)

McLeish, Norrie, *The Haunted Borders* (Alba Publishing, 1997)

Matthews, Rupert, *Haunted Edinburgh* (Pitkin, 1993)

Melville, Lawrence, *The Fair Land of Gowrie* (William Culross, 1939)

Prevost, W.A.J., *Annals of Three Dumfriesshire Dales* (Lockerbie Herald, 1954)

Robertson, James, *Scottish Ghost Stories* (Warner Books, 1996)

Scott, A. MacCallum, *Clydesdale* (Thornton Butterworth, 1924)

Seafield, Lily, *Scottish Ghosts* (Lomond, 1999)

Steven, Helen J., *The Cumnocks, Old and New* (Dunlop & Drennan, 1899)

Underwood, Peter, *Gazetteer of Scottish Ghosts* (Fontana, 1974)

— , *This Haunted Isle* (Harrap, 1984)

In addition to the above, the author has referred to various newspapers and magazines, old and new. Other information has been found in guidebooks to castles and mansions, on web sites and in brochures, as well as the personal accounts supplied by people who have witnessed spectres for themselves. In particular I wish to thank those people who told me their own experiences of spectres, poltergeists or hauntings, and many others who just happened to mention that 'this place is supposed to be haunted,' or something similar.

We do hope that you have enjoyed reading this large print book.

Did you know that all of our titles are available for purchase?

We publish a wide range of high quality large print books including:
Romances, Mysteries, Classics General Fiction Non Fiction and Westerns

Special interest titles available in large print are:
The Little Oxford Dictionary Music Book Song Book Hymn Book Service Book

Also available from us courtesy of Oxford University Press:
Young Readers' Dictionary (large print edition) Young Readers' Thesaurus (large print edition)

For further information or a free brochure, please contact us at:
Ulverscroft Large Print Books Ltd., The Green, Bradgate Road, Anstey, Leicester, LE7 7FU, England. Tel: (00 44) **0116 236 4325 Fax:** (00 44) **0116 234 0205**